How to Make Effective Sales in Retail Stores

ERKAN DEMIR

All rights reserved.

Erkan Demir

No part of this publication may be reproduced, distributed, or transmitted in any form or by any means, including photocopying, recording, or other electronic or mechanical methods, without the prior written permission of the publisher, except in the case of brief quotations embodied in critical reviews and certain other non-commercial uses permitted by copyright law. For permission requests, write to the publisher, addressed "Attention: Permissions Coordinator," at route785@gmail.com

About the book

While writing this book, I avoided using those fancy tables, graphics and pictures as they do in sales training manuals. I tried to be simple as much as I can. Since I come from sales background, I know what it takes to be a successful salesperson. Sales are learned from salespeople not from people who have never even sold a candy in their lives.

When I used to sell furniture, appliances and electronics, I used to have difficulties finding a sales book specializing solely on furniture and appliance sales. I self-taught myself most of subjects you will see in this book. I went into Google and learnt how to use humour in my sales, I went into Google I learned how to use the principle of reciprocity in my sales. I learned how to use compliments in my sales, I went into Google and learned how to learn from others including from the worst sales people etc. You will not have the most of the subjects you will read in this book in your training manual in your store. Therefore, I decided to write this book on appliances and furniture sales so you can benefit from my experiences and make the most money you can on the sales floor.

This could be the worst sales book you may read or this could be the best sales book you may read but if you can get the best sides of this book and apply them into your sales, I can guarantee you that you are going to make top money in your store.

You can also use this book in any retail store or in any sales job by applying some of techniques you will learn in this book.

TABLE OF CONTENTS

Chapter 1: The Sales

Chapter 2: How To Sell Yourself

Section 2.1 Be like chameleons

Section 2.2 Use the Principle of Likability

Section 2.3 Compliments

Chapter 3: The Importance of Humor in Sales

Chapter 4: The Sense of Touch in Sales

Chapter 5: The Importance of Personal Development

Chapter 6: How to Make Effective Sales Presentations

Chapter 7: Why Is Listening Important?

Chapter 8: Bad Sales Trainings

Section 8.1 Consequences of Bad SalesTrainings

Chapter 9: Why Is It So Important to Learn From Others?

Chapter 10: Why Is Role Playing So Important In Sales?

Chapter 11: The Topics You Should Never Share Or Discuss with your Co-workers

Chapter 12: How to Deal With Negative and Toxic Co-workers?

Chapter 13: How to be Resilient and How to be Overcome Customer Rejections?

Chapter 14: Important Personal Traits to be Succesful

Chapter 15: Difference Between Optimist and Positive Sales People

Chapter 16: Paradox of Choice

Chapter 17: Handling Promotions

Chapter 18: Customer Relations

Chapter 19: Financing

Chapter 20: Avoiding Returns

Chapter 21: How to Upsell and Cross-Sell

Chapter 22: Extended Warranty Sales

Chapter 23: The Principles of Persuasion

    Section 23.1 Social Validation

    Section 23.2 Authority

    Section 23.3 Reciprocity

    Section 23.4 Commitment

    Section 23.5 Likability

    Section 23.6 Scarcity

Chapter 24: The Six Step Selling Cycle

    Section 24.1 Greetings

    Section 24.2 Building Rapport

    Section 24.3 Discover Their Needs

    Section 24.4 Presentation

    Section 24.5 Objections

    Section 24.6 Closing

Chapter 25: The Summary

Chapter 1: The Sales

"Sales are contingent upon the attitude of the salesman – not the attitude of the prospect." – W. Clement Stone

> The sales is a process of persuasion to get a your customers to take action. Sales have always been present in our lives. For example, when a child wants candy or a toy, the child must try to persuade her parents. The child applies sales different sales techniques to persuade her parents. For example, she may smile, cry, sulk, or not even talk to her parents for a while.

In another example, when you date someone for the first time, you try to show your attractiveness and impress your prospective partner. Both of those scenarios are good examples how we become buyer or sellers in our lives without even thinking of it.

Sales have similarities with a chess game. For example, you try to read your customers' minds and emotions. You talk according to their responds as you do your moves according to your opponent's moves in a chess game.

In a typical sale process, you need to identify the needs and reveal the desires of the customers for your products. It is your goal for every customer to leave from your store with a successful purchasing experience. It is your responsibility to close a sale today not tomorrow.

I don't want to discourage you at the beginning of the book about commission-based sales jobs but I need to be upfront with you. Commission-based jobs are not for everybody. According to Art Sobczak, President of BusinessByPhone.com, commission-based jobs are good for people who:

- Hungry for knowledge
- Want to control their own salary
- Have an insatiable desire to succeed

According to him, best sales people:

- Must be motivated
- Self-disciplined
- Confident
- Positive

- A great interviewer and performer
- Have an immense desire to learn
- They should be someone who is never satisfied
- Have "I can do more attitude", and I can do better attitude

"The secret of getting ahead is getting started." -Mark Twain

---

Chapter 2: How to Sell Yourself

I am starting the second chapter with how to sell yourself because if *you know how to sell yourself first, you can sell anything you want*. There are different ways to sell yourself to your customers. Let's check these four are:

A. Building a personal relationship with your customers

B. Be like chameleons

C. Use the Principle of Likability

D. Compliments

A. Building a personal relationship with your customers:

Probably, you may not realize it, but so much of the quality of your life is tied to social interaction and personal relationships. Having successful relationships with your customers and being able to connect with them you come across on a daily basis all play a role in having a successful sales career. To be able to persuade any customer to buy your products, the first thing, you must know how to sell yourself to them. Therefore, you must know how to build a personal relationship with them. You should be like chameleons for each customer. As a professional salesperson, I know firsthand how it is important to connect with customers. Building personalized relationships is a key to sell almost anything to your customers. Forget about the product knowledge, forget about how to do an effective presentation, forget about how to overcome objections etc. Knowing your customers lets you in on the secrets of what your customers love to see and what annoy them. It gives you an insider perspective on their personal state that you need. Selling yourself starts with building personalized relationship with your customers. In order for you to understand better, I compiled some of vital subjects so that you can understand what you can do to build a personal relationship with your customers and sell yourself to them.

B. Be like chameleons:

"I like being like a chameleon who transforms himself with each role."-Oscar Isaac

Chameleons are amazing creatures; they change their colours according to their mood and according to their environment to escape from predators. The best sales people are social chameleons are champions when it comes to making a good impression. They never hesitate to practice the kind of emotional mercantilism where they hide their own feelings, thoughts, and opinions in order to be accepted and get the approval of from their customers. They blend into any customer with ease and they change their behaviours, their sales pitch, their sales presentations and they apply different sales techniques and use different tricks for each customer differently. They know each customer is unique and different.

As salesperson, you should always try to adapt and understand your customers' emotions, and their lives. In other words, you should speak their language. To survive in this competitive sales environment, you need to be phenomenal adapters like chameleons. You must learn how to blend seamlessly into any social sales environment, into any customer, and into any sales scenario.

In a research completed by Dr. Martin Kilduff, Professor of organizational behaviour at the University of Cambridge, have found that chameleon people move into central positions within social networks and enjoy early promotions in their careers. According to him, they always win people over by assuming the characteristics of whomever they are dealing with. These social chameleons often succeed in unfavourable environments and can achieve unexpected heights in their careers.

You should be an enthusiastic about each customer, be curious and approach each customer differently. For example, some customers may like that you use humour in your sales and some may not like it. You cannot joke with all customers. It may work on a previous sale but it does not give guarantee that it is going to work in your next sale. You need to change your pitch and behaviours for each customer by knowing the golden rule: each customer is unique and different. Each customer is truly one of a kind. Don't be like salespeople who pitch their products the same way over and over again. Be like a basketball coach. Change your sales tactics, your mimics, your emotions and your strategies for each customer differently.

Be like chameleons: be changeable and be adaptable!

C: Use the Principle of Likability:

This principle is also named as familiarity and sympathy at different sources. You probably have heard many times that people do business with people they know, they like and they trust.

According to Dr. Cialdini, people like doing business with people who have physical attractiveness, similarities, and people who give them good compliments.

In other words, people love doing business with salespeople who share common traits with them. In addition that those customers generally make judgements based on salespeople's external characteristics like their dress, and physical appearances. As salesperson, you can induce a sense of similarity with almost any customer by finding things you have in common with them to talk about. Customers are more likely to comply with requests made by salespeople that they like. If you can make them like you, then you have already sold yourself. Let's see what you can do to make them to like you.

> THE PRINCIPLE OF LIKABILITY IS DIVIDED INTO THREE:
> 1. Similarities
> 2. Compliments
> 3. The physical attraction and appearance

1: Similarities(Familiarities)

People have greater tendency to accept the proposals of people with whom they share common features and traits. We like people who are similar to ourselves and who have the same opinions, lifestyle, personality traits, age, race, origin, associations etc.

As professional salesperson, you should detect skilfully your common traits with your customers. Your customers will like to talk about things that you have in common with them. Finding something in common with your customers always leads a positive response by your customers and arise their automatic sympathy about you.

Some of similarity examples to find out and to talk about:

1. Talking about hobbies:

People love talking about their hobbies. If you have a customer who likes fishing, why not make him to talk about fishing. Even if you went to fishing once in your life, you can talk about your store. By asking him questions about fishing, you can make him talk about fishing. Let them talk more than you. They love talking about their hobbies.

2. Talking about sports:

Most of people like sports. They may be interested in going to gym, in body building, team sports like basketball, hockey, baseball, soccer or they may be interested in hiking, walking, skiing, skating etc...

Maybe there was an important hockey game last night and your customer's team won the game. You can talk about the game and show your interest about the game even if you did not watch it.

If your customer goes to gym to build a body, make him talk about his experiences about body building or if your customer is on diet to lose weight, make her to talk about her experiences. Both of these types of people love talking about those. Give them a chance to speak by asking a quick and short question and let them talk: I want to lose weight too. I have tried once but I have failed. What can you recommend me to lose weight? She will see that you are very curious about her weight lost diet and she will open up more.

3. Language:

Who would not like to be heard hello or how are you in their language in a foreign country? Since I have had a lot of immigrant friends and I have travelled a lot, I learned some words in different languages so I used to say a few words to immigrants in their native language. They loved that.

For example, if they were Chinese, I was saying hello

with a smiley face "Nǐ hǎo", I was saying "privet" to Russians and "Hallo", Wie geht es dir? to Germans etc.

Since I could speak some Spanish, with the customers from the South America, I used to speak to Spanish. These type of customers love to hear a few words in their language.

4. Geographical area of origin:

As salesperson, you can also look for a link such as being born in the same city with the customer, or having visited, having friends or relatives there where your customer moved from or was born.

It is a multicultural word. People move from countries to countries to pursuit a better life for themselves. They also move around their country.

Who would not like talking about their country especially when they live in another country? Or would not you like that someone knows your old city?

With the customers from the countries I been to, I was talking about my experiences in their country and making them to talk about their country. I also used to talk about their food, drinks, culture and customs.

For example, I used to talk about Ouzo with Greek customers which are a national drink of Greece which is also a national drink in Turkey or I used to talk about Chinese cuisine with Chinese customers and used to tell them what I liked about Chinese food etc.

It is not only country of origin but also you can also talk about their previous city. Sometimes, you will have customers who just moved from another city and you either lived in that city before or maybe you have a relative living over there. These types of customers like to compare two cities and they usually miss their previous city. Make them talk what they like and they don't like in this new city. If your customer moved from Toronto, tell him: I liked Toronto. I was at CN Tower and it was gorgeous. What were you doing in Toronto? What did take you here? Subjects will open subjects and they will spill out.

5. Profession:

Talking about their profession could be a good idea to find common ground to personalize with your customers to build a rapport.

For example, the Province of Saskatchewan in Canada

is known a depot of pulses in the world. We had a lot of farmer customers and they live far from everything. It was very hard to break the barrier with them. Fortunately, I had self-interest about pulses especially in lentils.

So I used to know a lot about lentils and its current prices. Since we had a lot of farmer customers in our store, I used to talk about pulses with them which they liked to talk about. We used to talk about current prices, how much hectare they have, if the season is going well for them etc...

6. Travel:

People love talking about talking travel and their experiences. Have you ever gone to Mexico? Have you ever been to Jamaica? Just ask these types of questions and let them talk.

I closed a big sale just by talking about travel. I had a customer who was going to visit Germany next week. I had been to Germany three times and I talked to him about my experiences in Germany and answered his questions. After I saw that he was in buying mood, I sold him over $6,000 furniture package.

7. Talking about familiarities (friends, places etc.)

You may have some familiar friends or people you know with your customers. You can talk about them in a positive way. Don't say any bad things about those familiar people. In addition that they may not like the person you want to talk about. In addition to familiar names, you may have also gone to the same school or somewhere like gym together with your customer in the past.

8. Show your curiosity:

> *"We keep moving forward, opening new doors, and doing new things, because we're curious and curiosity keeps leading us down new paths."-Walt Disney*

According to studies, people who are curious are often viewed in social encounters as more interesting and engaging, and they are more apt to reach out to a wider variety of people. In addition, being curious about your customers seems to protect you from negative sales experiences, like rejection, which could lead to better connection with your customers over time. Even if you do not have shared a common interest with your customer, show your customers that you are curious about their interest.

Albert Einstein explained his genius when he famously said, "I have no special talents. I am only passionately curious. "According to studies published in Greater Good Magazine find out that curious people have better relationships with others and connect better with others. In fact, other people are more easily attracted and feel socially closer to people that display curiosity.

You must be curious about their lives, their work, their hobbies, their appearance etc. and take them as your advantage to close your sale. You must be interested in them not in yourself when they are in your store.

For example, I had a customer who was a wrestler. I did not have any clue about this sport but I was interested in his story.

I showed him my curiosity in the wrestling and made him talk. He spoke out and told about the wrestling in excitement. I kept eye contact, asked short questions, mirrored his speech and showed him that I am listening to you. When I saw that he was in buying mood, I sold him with no objections.

D. Compliments:

"I can live for two months on a good compliment."

-Mark Twain

Giving compliments to your customers captures them directly by their ego. Compliments are definitely are effective to make them like you. You should be careful not to cross the line when you give compliments. Make sure that you do not do compliments about a race, ethnicity or religion. For example, I had a Chinese salesperson who supposedly wanted to give his customer compliment but that turned into a disaster. He told a Native American customer that he had a lovely T-Shirt with a smile. The customer had a Native war figures in his T-Shirt and thought that salesperson was teasing with his race. He became so angry and used heavy vulgar words to salesperson. Chinese salesperson did not intend anything bad about his race but he still made a mistake. I had another salesperson who said his customer: I have not seen you for long time. You have changed a lot. You look gorgeous but you have gained a lot of weight. You should lose some weight.

This was her conservation opener with customer. She crossed her line. Customer felt uncomfortable and was embarrassed. She did not say anything negative to her but you could see her irritation from her face impressions. She left without buying.

You also can give compliments to your customers about their success about their businesses:

For example, you deal with a customer who has a famous restaurant in the town. You can say him in excitement: I do love eating at your place. I do love everything you offer and your customer service is excellent. I was at your place last week and I ate a pizza with cedar salad.

> When you give compliments to your customers, you also have to make sure that you do not fake compliments.

For example, I had a customer who walked 15 minutes to come to our store in an heavy snowfall. One of salespeople said: hey you look so great and energetic today. Customer asked him: am I dumb or are you dumb? I had already been angry because my car had broken down and you were teasing with me.

You can also praise your customers publicly. For

example, you saw one of your teachers. You can tell your co-workers that she was my teacher at high school and she was the best teacher I had.

Some of the compliments I used in my sales that you can easily apply in your sales:

- If the customer says I am very old, you look so young and you look so energetic. They love hearing when you mean that they are young.

- If you see a customer with a great body, you can say: You look so fit, how you managed to have that great fit body?

- You see a customer with white teeth and you say: Having white teeth is my desire. I wish I had sparkling gorgeous white teeth as you have. I do everything to have white teeth like yours but I have not been successful. What is your secret?

- You see a customer with a classy dress and you say with a funny way: Am I or are you a salesperson? You look better than me with this classy dress.

- You see one of your old friends and telling her: oh my god, how beautiful you look today. You changed your hair style. You look gorgeous with this new hair style. Praising and complimenting your customers spur your likability. Receiving compliments from you, praising and flattering your customers can be very effective tool to provoke their feelings and buying from you.

3. The physical attraction and appearance

Would you continue dating with someone who looks shabby, dirty and smelly in the first date? You would not probably. A professional appearance will leave an immediate impression on your customers. The better you have a physical attraction and appearance, the more you will be liked by your customers. When you are physically attractive, it creates a positive effect on your customers. As you notice that attractive politicians, handsome or beautiful celebrities are more likely to be heard more than non-attractive ones. This rule applies in sales too. The physical attraction produces an "halo effect" because salespeople who are physically attractive are usually and unconsciously perceived with positive values such as success, transparency, and honesty. Having a good the halo effect with your customers, you can transfer your appeal to the products to sell. Having the physical attractiveness is a important influence to get yes from your customers. If you look shabby, wearing wrinkled dresses, it will be harder to attract them. In the professional sales world, looks are important and your first impression will last. Not only dressing well will not only increase your self-confidence but it will attract and influence your customers. A proper grooming, having clean and good dresses will give the impression your customers that you are a professional salesperson. Before coming to work, make sure that you have clean dresses on you, make sure that your hair does not look like you have just waken up. Make sure that you don't smell any type of odour. Prepare your work every morning as dancers prepare their dancing competition. Every day is a new day with new hopes and having a professional look will contribute to your sales numbers.As a professional salesperson, you must present yourself to your customers as the best possible as possible. Money brings money. Buy nice classy dresses. Invest on yourself first so your customers can invest on you.

What can we learn from a schizophrenic person to build a personalized rapport?

Ali is a schizophrenic person. He is heavily medicated. This serious disorder affects his thoughts, his actions and his behaviours. He stayed in a mental hospital for four years. He burnt his house down. He attempted suicide. He jumped from the fourth floor of a mental hospital. When he was asked why he jumped, he said: I saw other two roommates jump so I followed them and I jumped too. Both were killed but I was not killed. I was smart enough not to fall on my head while they fell on their head and were killed instantly. If he does not take his drugs, he becomes aggressive. He is a lucky person though. His two brothers take care of him and provide all his needs. Ali has an important trick to teach us: how to build a personalized rapport. Ali hangs out in a cafe every day. He is a loyal customer but he does not have enough money to pay for his drinks. He smokes over two pack cigarettes. To be able to find money to eat at restaurants, Ali has tricks and tactics: Ali knows how to ask for money to different people. If he sees certain people every day, he asks for money directly. For example, if he sees me every day and he asks me money without trying to building rapport with me and does not even care asking me how I am doing. Because he knows I don't eat his tricks (I sometimes give him anyhow). I am not a stable person for him to get money. However, if he sees a new person or a person after long time, he knows how to get money from them. He sits on the table and chats with him. He asks him how he has been, he makes jokes, and he talks about their past days together. He is very good at personalizing. He uses even touch sense by tapping on his shoulder quickly and saying: you look great even after all these years passed. He even uses reciprocity principle by offering him a tea or a smoke. Subject leads to subject and when it is the right time for him, he asks money. He says I will buy a pack smoke and I need some money to get a T-Shirt (or something else). Can you give me some money please? The person gives him money without hesitation. He gets what he wants and leaves with a thank you. These types of people give him more money also since he spent time with them and built a personal rapport with them. He never makes negative face impression if he is rejected by them. He never swears at the person. Because he knows he will ask money again. Ali is a great example on how to build rapport. He knows how to build a personalized rapport with strangers or people he has not seen for long time. He finds shared grounds and common things to talk about. Do what he does: build a personal rapport with your customers. Talk in your customers' language. Sell yourself first, not your products.

Chapter 3: Using Humour in Sales

> *"Your attitude is like a box of crayons that colour your world. Constantly colour your picture grey, and your picture will always be bleak. Try adding some bright colours to the picture by including humour and your picture begins to lighten up."*-
> Allen Klein

Using humour is definitely one of the most important principles to build a personalized relationship with your customer. I used humour in almost all of my sales. Customers buy from salespeople they like, and using humour in your sales is the easiest and fastest way to make them like you. When you use humour, and make your customers smile or laugh, it generates sympathy on them about you and it makes them more willing to listen to you. It also makes easier to sell them and improves your relationship with them.

It transmits your positive feelings to your customers and it improves their mood in a positive way. When your customers are relaxed, they will trust you more and they will share more personal information with you. It is very powerful way to put your customers in a good mood.

I have met tons of salespeople who were like politicians. They were like robots. They were too serious with customers like politicians, they did not have any emotions, they did not have any smile, they did not have any humour and they were very formal with their customers.

According to comedian and author Burt Teplitzky, using humour when you are trying to sell a product or service can have excellent results. Using humour and making moderate jokes help salespeople establish a bond with customers, it release tensions and increase your credibility.

He adds that salespeople's main task must be creating a positive environment to open channels of communication between you and your customers. If you can open these channels, you and they can communicate with each other more comfortably.

Humour has power to change people's opinions, and it reinforces what they think or feel. Humour also could help you break ice with difficult customers or with angry customers.

When you apply humour in your sales, avoid to talk:

-Race, religion, body weight, politics.

If you don't use humour correctly, it can give a negative effect. Don't be like those annoying or "cool" comedians who are not creative to find subjects to joke about and who only use race issues in their comedies.

I will give you three examples so you can know what your lines are not to cross:

1. **Don't use any humour about races:** I had a salesperson who had thought that his customer was from India. He had told his customer: You guys always had had problems with Pakistan and I supported you against Pakistan. Well, he was from Pakistan. He did not say anything bad to the salesperson but salesperson was so ashamed when he learnt he was from Pakistan.

2. **Don't use humour about their body weights:** I had a salesperson who told customer: be careful, you will break the mattress with your body weight. Customer felt so offended and embarrassed. She said I have to go and she left without saying anything.

3. **Don't use humour about their appearances**: I had

another salesperson who said his customer: you have a lot of grey hair. Customer felt so pissed off and of course he did not buy.

Summary:

Humour is very effective sales tool. If you want to make a sale, you need to be like friends with your customers as if you had known each other for years. Using humour in your sales will increase personal relationship and you credibility.

A genuine smile can make huge difference and humour is a way to make them smile quickly. If you can transfer your energy to your customers with humour, you will have a bonded relationship with them that means they will buy from you more willingly.

> "A sense of humor is part of the art of leadership, of getting along with people, of getting things done." – Dwight D. Eisenhower

Chapter 4: The Sense Touch in Sales

Touch is essential to the human experience. There are two types of touches you in sales settings in retail:

1. Touching on customers
2. Letting your customer touch and hold products

"Touch seems to be as essential as sunlight."-Diane Ackerman

In many commercial settings, casually touching customers has been shown to increase the time they spend on shopping and increasing tips at restaurants.

According to Michael Lynn from Cornell University's research increases tips at restaurants. Customers with a small and quick touch from shoulder by waitresses increased average tip of from 12% to 14%.

There are different ways to use the sense of touch with your customers. For example, you already built very good rapport with your customer. He told you that he gained some weight recently. With a simple tap on his shoulder by saying him: you look gorgeous and you can make it lose again will increase the odds to your requests to sell your products. You have to be careful who to tap on shoulder. Don't do that if you still have barrier with your customers.

If you are a male, only touch on males. If you are female, touch only on females and only do a small tap on their shoulders. Your touch must be hardly noticed by your customers. It must be placed in right time and right way.

Otherwise, even a simple tap on their shoulders may cause harm even if you made it with the best intent. Touching them releases an happy chemicals and serotonin in their brains. It also lowers their cortisol levels (the stress hormone), reduces their feelings of stress, and reduces disputes.

You can also touch on your customers when you apology for something or when you share their sadness. Touching during an apology and making empathy about their sorrow adds warmth and sincerity.

If you aware of what your customers truly feel and

having knowledge of how to react their emotions or their situations can result in increase in your sales and the sense of touch could be a great to tool to influence your customers.

Letting your customers touch and hold products:

Do you know that touch can significantly influence the perception that the consumer has about a product?

In 2003, The State of Illinois issued a statement around the Christmas holidays and they warned consumers to be careful about holding an object because it might encourage them to buy it

Joann Peck from University of Wisconsin and Suzanne B.Shu from UCLA wondered if the warning was valid and if really touching a product influences our decisions to buy.

In their research, they found out that that warning from the state is valid. In their studies, they found out that touching an object increases the feelings of ownership for people and they feel like buying it.

Apple could be a great example in retails for touching. Apple displays their sample products in a smart way for you to touch and to play with them.

How can we take advantage the sense of touch to sell?

Apple allow customers to touch without salespeople, customers enter their store and touch Apple products on their own. There is no salesperson involved in usually when customers touch and play with the products.

You don't work at Apple but you can encourage your customers to touch products in your store and let them play with them, let them sit on or lay on products.

Physically holding and touching your products by your customers can create a sense of psychological ownership. It also influences the amount that a customer is willing to pay for a product.

As salesperson, you should always seek is to promote positive feelings. When the prospective buyer sees the product, you should let him he touch it.

If you are selling dishwasher, let customer touch the product, let him touch, play with buttons, let him open the lid. If you sell mattress, let customer lay on mattress, if you sell chair, let customer sit on it. Uses their touch sense to feel the product and make them fell they own it already.

I used to ask my customers, would you buy a car without doing a test drive? They always say no, well, you will probably use your mattress more than anything in your life. So, please lay on mattress to try it. You don't sit seven hours constantly on sofa, you don't watch TV seven hours non-stop, you don't drive seven hours non-stop and you don't walk seven hours non-stop but you sleep average seven hours on the mattress non-stop if you don't give a short washroom break or if you don't have a nightmare.

Like your walking shoes, your mattress is very important for you. Please lay on it and try it. I want you to feel mattress. Please touch and squeeze the mattress to see how you feel about its quality and firmness.

I will give another good example how a car dealer hired me right away at job interview:

I had an interview at a major Ford dealer in a small town. There were general manager and two sales managers in the interview room. They asked me classical interview questions that I answered properly.

The general manager asked me that I will hire you if you manage to sell me the chair you are sitting on. I said sure I can sell you that chair.

I invited him to sit on chair and I explained why the chair is good for him. I asked him to get up and sit down again and move around chair. After he sat more on it, I told him can you feel that the chair is very comfortable and it makes you sit all time and smiled smoothly. You are also lucky, this chair goes fast and we have only left for you. You know your friend Jack? He was here last week. He had bought this chair because he liked the softness of the chair.

He told me that is enough. You are hired. He asked me: do you know why I hired you?

I said I know why but I want to hear it from you. He said you used my touch sense and made me sit on chair to make me feel like I already own this chair.

I will give you another example from a Gypsy saleslady who was selling flowers on the street:

Gypsy flower saleslady:

I went to Istanbul for a vacation and sat down at an outdoor cafe. This neighbourhood was preferred by young couples as it had lots of cafes. While waiting for my order, I saw a Gypsy lady selling flowers in the centre of the cafes. If she came across someone walking alone, the Gypsy saleslady did not bother to talk to them; however, when she saw a young couple holding hands, she quickly approached them, placing the flowers in the guy's hands and began doing her sales pitch. Even if the guy did not want to hold the flowers, he did so as he was too embarrassed to return them to the saleslady.

The saleslady was very successful at what she did. After he holds the flowers, the saleslady gives one to the girl. She was making both of them smell the flowers at the same time saying: You look like these flowers; you smell nice, look classy and you match with each other perfectly. She said to the girlfriend: I wish I had a boyfriend like him. She managed to sell to four out of five couples in 25 minutes. Her tactics and her pitch were impressive. She was not aggressive. She was smiling in her pitch. She had great persuasion skills. She used humour and she used touch and smell senses to sell.

When I was leaving, I told her that she was a great salesperson. What is your most important trick? She said, the most important trick is that when they touch my flowers, it is harder for them to resist not buying them. Once they hold it, they feel they own the product already and when they smell the flowers, they love the smell and buy it without question. She is another great example how using touch sense can help us in our sales.

Summary:

When you buy clothes, you touch, when you buy apples, you touch, then you should let your customer touch on products. Do not let your customers look at products in distance. If you sell a chair, pull the chair in front of customer and let him sit instead of pointing chair to let him sit. Customers will feel like obligated to sit. If you sell sectional, move pillows around and let them sit. If you sell TV, give remote control to your customers and let them change channels.

You will see there will be big chance in your sales

numbers if you can adapt touch sense into your sales.

"Joann Peck and Suzanne B. Shu. "The Effect of Mere Touch on Perceived Ownership." Journal of Consumer Research: October 2003.

Chapter 5: The Importance of Personal Development

"Formal education will make you a living; self-education will make you a fortune." — *Jim Rohn*

"I think I have improved from last year. I am always trying to improve my game and improve myself."
Cristiano Ronaldo

Do you want to get better at a certain skill? Do you want to be the best salesperson? Do you want to make money? If your answer is yes, then you must continue pushing yourself to the limit by improving yourself and developing new skills.

Personal development is one of the most important tools to progress yourself in your sales career. It is like a fuel to add in your gas tank to take you from the bottom to the top.

The sales are a demanding, challenging and stressful job. With personal development and with self-improvement, you can certainly get better through your sales career.

According to Art Sobczak, the salespeople who earn the highest commission generally practice self-improvement regimens. "The superstars are hard workers and realize it's not a 'get rich quick' profession. They are the ones who are constantly trying to do better by learning, researching and getting to know their product and customers. Salespeople never graduate from the school of sales. There is always more to be learned." If you're not willing to learn and if you are not hungry for knowledge, you are less likely to succeed in sales.

I will give you two real examples how personal development can grow you and when you lack of it, how it can take you down.

In the summer of 2002, two teenager wingers from Portugal started to appear in European football.

Both were playing for Sporting CP. They were Ricardo Quaresma and Christiano Ronaldo.

Quaresma was considered to have more natural talent and having more core football skills than Ronaldo by football authorities. He went to Spain to play for Barcelona and Ronaldo went to England to play for Manchester United.

In England, Ronaldo started to improve himself every

day. He sucked his Scottish manager Fergusons' yells. He abided by the hierarchy of the team's dressing room and allowed himself to adapt and learn other best players' lifestyle and game skills in the team.

He learnt the Scottish player Gig's dribbling, the Dutch player Nistelrooy's movements, Roy Keane's passions, and his manager's discipline.

After Manchester United, he went to Spain to play for Real Madrid. He continued to push the limits in Real Madrid too. His Portugal National Team manager said about his development and willingly to learn new skills and tricks:

"I have always spent time with players on free-kicks but with Ronaldo we worked for days and days. We practised every day. There's nobody who's prepared to work harder for his artistry".

His Portugal National Team manager also said:

"There are some great players that have so much belief that when things are not going well on the training field they just stop. They think, 'I am good, today is not right, but tomorrow it will be fine.' They never think there could be a problem. Not Cristiano.

He works and works until everything goes right and only then is he satisfied."

Ronaldo also spent hours in the gym to develop his skills with intensive trainings. He did not stop when he became one of the best. He still works hard to develop himself to stay on the top. He is considered one of the best players in football history.

Let's continue Quaresma's story:

After joining Barcelona, Quaresma's development started to stall. He started to fight with his teammates. He did not listen to his manager's tactics. He started to see himself that he was above the team and wanted to have free role in games. His neighbours even joined together and protested to him due to loudly house parties at his home. He asked even his neighbours: how much did your home worth? I would all of your homes and you would leave from here. He had too much ego. He thought he was the best but he was wrong. He failed in Spain.

After he failed in Barcelona, he went to Italy, England, Portugal and Turkey to play for different teams. He failed to show his talents at these countries too. He is considered as a wasted gift in football history. Meanwhile, Ronaldo has continued to go up in his career. He went to Italy to play for Juventus FC in 2018. His transfer fee alone was €120 million for four years.

"If you think you're perfect already, then you never will be" Cristiano Ronaldo

Summary:

You must strive to be better than yesterday. Any new day is an opportunity to make more money and to a step towards to be the best.

If Ronaldo still pushes himself to be the best, then you should if you think that the sales will be your career. Ronaldo makes about €35 million yearly and Quaresma makes about €2 million. Be like Ronaldo not like the latter one.

Learning any new sales skills or learning more about your products will be more extra cards in your pocket to show your customers and they will increase your credibility, authority, and will fill your pocket.

Chapter 6: How to Make Effective Sales Presentations

There is a natural flow in any sales presentations and stakes are high for you to have an effective and influential presentation.

I compiled some important points for you during the presentations below:

A. Eye contact:

There is an old saying that "eyes are a reflection of your inner self". There can be many different meanings to eye contact.

Eyes contacts increase qualities of interactions with your customers. Eye contacts reveal their thoughts and feelings. Keeping eye contacts also demonstrate them that you pay attention to them.

While keeping eye contact with them, you should avoid having continuous eye contact. It could be considered as rude behaviour by some customers.

According to Carol Kinsey Gorman author of The Silent

Language of Leaders, you should do just the right amount of eye contact with people. The right amount eye contact produces a feeling of mutual likability and trustworthiness.

She says that between 30%-60% eye contact is ideal during your conservation. Lastly, you should break off your eye contact after 5 seconds.

B. Face to them:

When you talk to your customers, make sure that face to them. Do not look around, do not talk to others sales associates or customers, do not check your phone if you receive a text message or a call. You should solely focus on your conservation with them.

Keep the distance with them when you are having a face-to-face conservation with them. Don't be too close nor don't be too far from them. Keep 7-9 feet distance with your customers. Some customers don't like if you are too close to them.

C. Minimize external distractions:

A brief interruption by your co-workers or most importantly from other customers can cause you to lose the thread of what you have been talking to your customers and even interruptions can cause to lose a sale.

According to Erik Altman from Michigan State University, even 2-3 seconds interruptions by others are long enough to lose thread. Brief interruptions also will greatly increase mistakes made.

Before making your presentation, try to find a quiet spot far from distractions, noise, and make sure that you and your customers don't block other customers and other sales people' walking path.

I have worked with salespeople who were jumping in each other's presentations by being noisy because they were doing the presentations too close to each other.

For example, I had a salesperson who was so noisy about other salespeople' presentations. With any mistake a salesperson makes, she used to go to manager about the salesperson's mistakes during the presentation.

Not only other salespeople can interrupt your presentation but also sometimes other customer can interrupt you by asking something or they may be noisy with your conservation with your customers and jump into conservation.

Your customers may argue even with each other if you are too close to other customers.

I had a salesperson whose customers argued with another salesperson's customers about the politics because the salesperson was doing his presentation next to a couple who was also involved in the same product. You should wait for your turn if other sales associate is doing his/her presentation at the product you want to show your customers. Do not let other customers hear what you are talking with your customers.

In addition to all above, if you do your presentation at somewhere centred in your store, other customers can see you and your customers. It does happen that your customers' friends or some acquaintances show up and interrupt your presentations. I know this is so annoying but it does happen.

I will give you a last example why doing presentations from other salespeople could be a good idea for you.

I had salesperson. He was the best salesperson in the store. Well, it was me. Of course, who else could be? English is my second language as you may guess and I got accent.

I was trying to sell electric smooth-top range to my customer. The customer had bought a mattress a month ago from me so I knew him. I had an amazing rapport built with him so selling him a range was as if selling a candy. I planted the seeds in the middle of the sale to sell extended warranty, and when I found that he was going to buy. I started to explain our extended warranty.

I told him:

If smooth-top is broken, our extended warranty covers it. I did not mean that customer physically breaks it but I meant if smooth-top stops working.

A noisy salesperson was listening our conservation interrupted our conservation by saying: no, if he breaks it, our warranty does not cover it. He pays for it! I said kindly: Thanks for following our presentation and trying to correct me but I did not mean a physical break. I meant if it stops working because of malfunction. She said that when you say, if it breaks down, he understands that physical break like hitting on it or drop something on it and crack it.

Customer interrupted and said her with an angry voice: thanks for disturbing us, we are fine and I understood what he had meant so she stopped. He still bought the oven with 4 years warranty.

This shows us how it is important to make your presentation far away than others. If you see your co-workers close to you, take your customers to somewhere farther from them, or if you have customers close to you, go a little farther. After this sour event, I always tried to do my presentations far from others.

Lastly, when I used to use cash register to ring the sales, I always tried to use a cash register far from distractions because I sometimes used to pitch the warranty quickly to customers if I could not sell the warranty before closing the sale. I always used to try one more time in cash register. I used to show the customers on the screen what they were buying and I was changing my pitch to sell warranty with a different technique. I sold so many warranties at my second attempt on cash register.

Small trick: When you ring your sale, pull out a chair for your customer to sit down while you are processing the sale. A bar stool would be ideal way to make them sit. When they sit, they get relaxer and if you could not sell extended warranty at first, letting them sit on chair will make them relaxer and you can pitch the warranty one more time quickly.

D. Mirroring:

Mirroring is reflection technique that consists of body language, speed of words, and volume of the voice, gestures and imitating postures.

Mirroring your customers make them feel comfortable, making them to acknowledge your presence and giving them impression that you and they are similar to each other. In addition that it also creates a positive feeling and responsiveness in your customers that help you builds a good rapport with them. Mirroring increases customer's confidence on us and it gives us advantage to be close with the customer to make suggestions. Mirroring is one of the most important proven sales tools to showing and receiving empathy and increases your chances to be accepted by your customers.

Some of examples of mirroring:

- If you're using gestures when speaking, you respond with similar gesture.
- If your customer sits on the sofa, you sit on sofa.
- If the cross their hands, you cross your hands.

Mirroring in speaking can help you create suggestions and you can use these suggestions to close your sale.

For example, you have a customer and he is interested in buying a dryer. I like your dryer more than X but I am concerned about high price. You mirror what he says: What you are saying that I like your dryer more than X but I am concerned about price.

When you do this, customer will immediately have more closeness with you and he will be open to any suggestion. And you will immediately offer your suggestion and put your opinion to overcome his objection.

When you do mirroring, you should try to act natural

and keep fine balance. If you go too far in mirroring, you will make them feel like you are mocking and mimicking them. Match their tone, match them voice. You will see that mirroring will help you improve your sales.

Chapter 7: Why is Listening Important?

"Most people do not listen with the intent to understand; they listen with the intent to reply."- Stephen R. Covey

Listening is one of the most important fundamentals in sales. It is generally believed that selling is just talking and a good salesperson typically considered is a good talker.

However it is totally a wrong assumption. The ability to listen to your customers has proven to be an effective tool that will have a great impact on your sales.

During listening, you must know what you are doing. I compiled some of vital points during the listening. Let's check them below now.

1. Make Eye Contact:

Having eye contact is so important when you listen to your customers. Looking the customer in eye increase customers' connection with you and they make them feel important. It also makes customers feel recognized, understood and validated.

<u>Note</u>: Don't focus too hard, glance every three to five

second while doing it. You must also be aware of cultural differences. In some cultures when you do too much eye contact with women, it is considered a dating offer or rude.

2. Ask Questions:

Asking your customers questions during listening makes customer think that you care about them. As Theodore Roosevelt said, "People don't care how much you know until they know how much you care."

For example, if your customer is saying that her dishwasher stopped working, asking her questions about dishwasher will make her think that you care about her problem and you understand her situation.

3. Turn your body toward your customers:

When you speak and listen to your customers, turn your body toward them.

4. Show Empathy:

As in previous example, if your customer says that her dishwasher stopped working, then be emphatic with her. I am sorry to hear that you experienced this. I had the same problem when my x product stopped working or I had another customer who came and bought dishwasher because hers was also stopped working. Start with empathy and after that give them your solutions.

5. Don't interrupt and don't predict:

Salespeople often make assumptions even before customers finished speaking and they interrupt their customers. Interrupting your customers in mid-sentence during a conversation can trigger irritation by your customers and can be seen rude.

Don't also interrupt them by predicting what they are going to say. They may say something different than what you predicted and it can cause losing your credibility.

For example, if your customer says he works at pork plant and he got a quick permission from his boss to drop in your store to see mattresses, and if you interrupt and say: I know the owner of that plant. He is my customer and he is very nice customer of mine but he may not like his boss. Don't predict, and go with flow.

6. Focus on them not on your cell phone:

When you listen to them, don't check your cell phone. Your customer is with you and he wants you to pay him attention.

Don't annoy them by checking your cell phone all the time. Also, checking your cell phone will distract you and you may forget what he was talking about.

7. Avoid external distractions:

Try to be away from other salespeople, and from customers in the store. Don't block your customers' pathway. They may interrupt you and your customers. Try to find a quiet area on the busy sales floor.

8. Nod your head:

When you nod slowly, it shows you agree with your customers and it encourages them keep talking.

9. Match their facial expressions:

If you see they are concerned or worried, furrow your brow. If they seem unhappy, frown and lower your eyes.

Matching their facial expressions briefly will show your customers that you are listening and make them to trust you more.

10. Ask relevant questions:

When you listen to them, ask relevant follow up questions to understand their situation better. Keep asking these relevant questions to show them you are interested in them.

11. Give short feedback and reflect their speech:

By giving feedbacks what you just heard will increase the impression you are giving them. They will appreciate of your ability to listen to them by if you summarize the subject shortly. Reflect what you heard. Reflecting what said is better approach than asking them to repeat one more time.

12. Watch your body language:

Watch your body language when you listen to them. Even if you are bored with what you are listening, don't exhibit these body language behaviours:

- Looking at something or someone body else
- Turning your body away from them
- Giving them minimal or tense facial expressions

- Down-casting your eyes and maintaining a little contact with them.

Summary:

Listening to your customers is a basic human need. Customers want to see that you are listening to them. Listening to your customers actively will give you enough time and clues about your sales strategy and about your sales plan. It will also give you key opportunities to form a rapport with your customers.

Each customer is different so each sale requires a different strategy and tactics. In order to close your sale, don't miss valuable information they give you. Any extra information will be an extra opportunity to sell and more money in your next paycheque.

Chapter 8: Bad Sales Trainings

Salespeople can contribute to success of their company if they can be trained properly to perform their jobs.

According to Harward Business Review, U.S companies spend approximately $70 billion on trainings. To train salespeople, they spend $1,459 for per salesperson which is almost 20% more than in all other functions.

However, there are many disadvantages of sales trainings. I compiled some of vital shortcomings:

1. Inexperienced sales managers and bad managers:

I had times when I was trained by inexperienced sales managers or trainers who even had not sold a candy in their lives. I am sure that you will have some type of managers like above.

I am not saying that these two type of people cannot train you. Actually, these types of people know everything except sales. They are good at customer relations, they are friendly, they know their products well etc.

But they usually lack of sales skills. For example, I had a

sales manager who was training me. He never sold before and he had been a store manager at convenience store before.

He used to tell sales trainees: don't let customers leave from the store without buying (he is correct). If they want to buy mattress, show all of mattresses in the store until they buy it. Well, we had over 15 mattresses in the store. It will take at least two hours to show all of mattresses. *You do not do that. Ask relevant questions and always narrow your choices.* You are a sales person not a customer service representative. That sales manager was one of those type managers who hired to sales manager position because he knew the region manager.

I had a store manager who was so rude to customers and salespeople. She was yelled many times by customers. She did not have any respect among workers.

I had even a customer who swore at her when the store was full of customers. She had very bad name not only in her town but also in other towns. I used to work at competition in another city before working in this store that was 45 miles further. I had customers who used to drive 45 miles to buy furniture from us. I remember that I had a customer who drove 45 miles to us to buy a sectional because she was rude to him so he drove to us to buy a sectional. When I got a job offer at that store, my store manager told me not to go there because their store manager is so rude.

After working there, I saw that she was the worst manager I seen in my all of sales career without hesitation. She did not care about customers or salespeople. She hired people who were on drugs by knowing that they had used to take drugs including her husband's best friend who was on drugs with suicidal thoughts. She even argued with one customer because she thought that he was looking at her breasts.

Although she had bad interactions with customers and workers, she knew how to play office politics. When the region manager comes, she had her best clothes, and was taking out him for dinner. You will see tons of bad managers like her.

2. They don't have role-playing in trainings:

They teach everything from the company training manuals and from the company training website.

It is very useful to learn from these sources but salespeople are not given enough time to practise this newly acquired knowledge or skills with role plays in a controlled way before starting to sell. Sales managers can also see that new salespeople are ready or not ready to sell.

3. They don't provide customized training:

Most of companies allow salespeople to be mentored by one salesperson during the training.

Why not mix job shadowing with different salespeople rather than with making new trainee job shadowing with only one salesperson during the training.

If Charmaine is good at selling furniture but not good at selling appliances, why not also allow new sales trainee to shadow Alex who is better than Charmaine at selling appliances.

Why not allow the new sales trainee to adapt all of salespeople's strengths by job shadowing different salespeople during the training.

It is always better to hear different voices. If your mentor lies to his customers, it may affect your sales in the future because you will not be fully trained by a liar sales person even if he or she is the best in your store.

For example, if new salesperson Jessica is mentored by Jennifer who is known lying her customers, new salesperson may adapt her bad habits. If Jessica was mentored and did job shadowing different salespeople, she could see strengths of each salesperson and use their good sides in her sales in the future.

4. They don't have demographics training:

In addition that I never seen any company who provides specific demographics training for their salespeople. If the population of the town 10,000 and if 3000 of 10,000 people are immigrants, why not to have a short training about these immigrants' culture, customs, a few words in their language etc.?

If most of 3,000 immigrant population Chinese, why not hire one Chinese salesperson to attract more Chinese into the store?

The same sales training methods may not work will work the same in all locations.

Toronto foreign-born population by ethicity	
South Asian	12.59%
Chinese	11.3%
Black	8.91%
Filipino	5.67%
Others	7.63%

Look at Toronto example. If you lived in Toronto, 46.1% of your customers would be immigrants. Would not it be nicer to have a short training to attract these immigrants to your store? Would not be that a smart idea to teach salespeople some information about these immigrants?

If they don't provide this training, then as salesperson, you do it on your own and learn about majority of immigrants in your town. It may not make big difference if you live in a big city, but it does major difference in smaller cities. In smaller cities, immigrants are more connected with each other and they recommend places to each other to shop. I closed so many deals to immigrants by just learning a few things about their background. It does work!

In addition to demographic information, their layouts for the products are always the same. When I worked at one of my furniture places, Sears closed their location in the town. So we were the only company selling appliances after Sears' closure. We started to have many customers to buy appliances after Sears closure. We requested many times to our head office to remove three long bulky 8 chair dining tables from our display so we can extend our appliance department with more appliances to display. We could extend our appliance department more than half by removing those three dining tables but the company did not allow because they had agreement with table manufacturers to display their products in all over Canada.

We had also a coffee table with two stools in middle of mattress section among mattresses. We only sold piece in a year!

We requested to remove it and put one more mattress on the floor to display. Again, we could not get permission to display one more mattress. They had agreement to display it with manufacturer. If that coffee table with two stools is sold well in Toronto, it does not mean that it will be sold well in another city!

5. They don't focus on core skills:

When I worked at a leading furniture store, we had three weeks training. During these three weeks, they focused on product knowledge every day.

They did not have any focus on core fundamental sales skills such as presentation, questioning, building rapport, closing etc. They did not even have scarcity, reciprocity principles even their training manual. I had thought that I started to work at a candy shop for a moment. I had salesperson who did not even know what scarcity means in two years over there!

6. Boring sessions:

Some of retail companies organize boring training sessions during 8 hours every day with lunch and regular breaks. Trainer does presentations about company policies, products, sales principles etc. There is no involvement in these sessions by trainees; there are no prizes, no contests etc.

7. Wasted time:

The companies want you to absorb too much

information during the training. Some of the training subjects are not even actually used in sales floor which means they waste their time and money for the subjects that no salespeople use in real sales environment.

Consequences of bad sales trainings:

- Poor customer service and loss of customers

- Can you imagine dealing with a salesperson who does not even know how to greet customer because he was not trained properly?

- Untrained salespeople tarnish the company's brand and fame.

Some company trainings don't even teach how to overcome different customer objections like competition. For example, I had a co-worker who told the customer to go to competition when customer said this product was cheaper in the competition. I asked him why you told customer that. He said my manager in training told me: even if they go to competition, they will come back because we are the cheapest.

Some other important consequences of bad sales trainings:

Poor time management:

Lack of proper training will cause salespeople' speed to close the sales. They will take more time to close the sales that will make customers wait to be helped.

High turnovers:

There is a saying: Employees don't leave companies, they leave managers. This is totally true. The salespeople join companies but leave managers. According to a Gallup survey, number one reason why 1 million Americans changed their jobs by quitting was due to bad bosses or supervisors.

Salespeople who feel they did not have a good training and support after training, they may become frustrated and they will likely to look for opportunities elsewhere.

Employee morale:

When companies don't invest on salespeople, salespeople will be less willing to invest on them. If salespeople are not trained adequately, they will feel unsatisfied with their job and will be stressed out. Lack of training will also lead them to feel unappreciated.

When there is no enough support on sales floor, it will reduce their morale and their confidence in their job. They will likely turn into other salespeople to get help rather than asking managers that will make other salespeople frustrated too.

For example, I had a new co-worker who had two weeks short training. He often used to ask questions to other salespeople when he could not answer customers' questions.

He asked a question about a TV to another salesperson another salesperson about a fridge and he told him that you had asked me twice before, if I answer your question now, you have to share your commission with me. The salesperson felt so offended and went back to customer with empty hands.

Poor Performance:

When sales managers aren't adequately trained, it affects the performance of the new salespeople.

According to Gallup researchers, Dale Carnegie, and

Towers Watson, 70% of employees working with less performance and less effectively than their capacities because of bad managers.

Bad bosses cause companies to lose revenues, and growth opportunities, but good bosses make revenue growth if they can satisfy their employees.

For example, according to Anthony J. Rucci, Steven P. Kirn and Richard T. Quinn's Performance Measurement research, when Sears increased employee satisfaction by 5%, customer satisfaction improved by 1.3%, which led to a .05% improvement in revenue. Their total revenue then was $50 billion. In another words, Sears made extra $250 million revenue by improving their workers' working conditions in 1998.

Summary:

Lack of training reflects quality of management in the companies. If there are high turnovers, the managers should question their training and their behaviours first. Poor trained salespeople are will likely experience poor productivity.

At this point, salespeople will leave or to be fired

because of low productivity. However, hiring new salesperson will he more costly than retraining existing salesperson.

Sales managers, store managers, HR managers must work themselves instead of holding salespeople accountable. They should listen to the ideas of salespeople and engage with them during and after training.

Sales trainers with no sales background should not train new salespeople, and HR managers with no sales background should exclude writing sales training manuals and they should stop dictating what salespeople should learn except company policies.

Chapter 9: Why Is It Important to Learn From Others?

You can always learn from other co-workers something that you don't have during the training and after the training. I want to focus on how you can learn from others with customized job shadowing. Job shadowing is a simply training process that a new salesperson follows and observes an experienced employee in real sales environment with the customers.

Job shadowing help new salesperson increasing his knowledge, sales skills and help the new salesperson to be familiar about the products, the computer system to ring the sale and his role in his new job.

Job shadowing is a very effective training method for sales jobs but there are some flaws of the job shadowing. All companies give you an experienced and usually top salesperson to shadow during your sales training. This approach is a completely wrong in job shadowing. I will tell you the reasons why job shadowing only one salesperson is wrong during the training. I made a table for you and put 10 sample strengths and weaknesses of four different salespeople. Of course, there are more than 10 weaknesses and strengths for these four salespeople but I did not make you confused and wanted to keep it simple.

Cathy:

Cathy: 7 years sales experience
Total sales up to 1st of June: $700,000
Annual target: $1,100,000
Gross Margin: %7
Extended Warranty rate: 5%
Average sale: $425, 00
Discount rate: 8.5%
Closing ratio: %15

Cathy

STRENGTHS	WEAKNESSES
Listening	Overcoming objections
Social validation	Warrant sales
Organized	Building value
Building rapport	Discounts
Follow-ups and networking	Team player
Product knowledge	Negativity, gossip and a continuous complainer
Likability	Self-motivation, hunger and passion

Work-life balance	Personal development
Resiliency	Competitiveness
Accountability	Upselling, cross-selling

Cathy:

She is top writer in the store. She has a personalized approach with her customers. She also asks her customers to give her referrals. She gets a lot of referrals from her customers that make her top writer in the store. She sells more than everybody but she drags the store to bottom in gross margin, discounts and warranty sales. She cannot persuade customers to buy warranty. She does not know well how to do cross-selling and upselling. Although she lacks of some core sales skills like those two, she is so hardworking person. She never comes to work late; she does all of her tasks without being asked. She also has negative personal traits and gossips a lot behind other co-workers especially Tim and Jennifer. She sometimes even complains about Tim to her customers which is very bad behaviour and not professional. Cathy hates Jennifer and calls her "shit disturber". She also hates Nicole and gossips behind her who is a store manager. She also does not know how to build value for the products and go to store manager Nicole a lot of times to allow her to give discounts for her customers. She even goes to Nicole to get discount for $50 worth chair. She does not have motivation and does not have eager to learn new sales tricks to improve her sales. She is very personable salesperson with her customers. She talks to her customers as if she has known them for years. 15% of her customers are old customers who have bought from her before. She is a resilient salesperson and if she cannot close a sale, she knows how to move on to next one. She does not find excuses why she could not close the sale. She knows that knowledge is power and product knowledge can mean more sales for her. She knows her products very well especially mattresses.She knows every detail of each mattress in the store and this knowledge brings her more mattress sales. She sells more mattress than anyone. Although she sells more mattress than anyone, she cannot sell mattress attachments because she does not know how to build value on mattress attachments as newer salesperson Tim does.

Jason:
Jason: 5 years sales experience
Total sales up to 1st of June: $500,000

Annual target: $1,000,000
Gross Margin: %6
Extended Warranty rate:5%
Average sale: $450,00
Discount rate: 8%
Closing ratio: %13
Jason:

STRENGTHS	WEAKNESSES
Multi-tasking	Resiliency
Listening	Building rapport
Tech-Savvy	Appearance
Team player	Self-Motivation, passion and hunger
Accountability	Competitiveness
Qualifying questions	Warranty sales, upselling, and cross-selling
Order taker	Overcoming objections
Time management	Work-life balance
Appearance	Empathy

Curiosity	Likability
Job commitment	Discounts

Jason:

Jason has worked for five years and he is the second most experienced salesperson after Cathy. He is an average salesperson. He does not have motivation, passion and hunger. He does to know how to build a personal relationship with customers. This guy is famous of blaming others for failures in his sales and he always finds excuses. He is not a resilient person and he becomes so sad if he cannot close a sale. But when he comes to the product knowledge, he knows his products very well like Cathy. He is the best salesperson in the store knowing about electronics and appliances. He knows everything about TVs and appliances since he has personal interest in electronics and appliances.

He is too formal with customers. Although he knows about his products, he forgets to be a salesperson and tries to educate his customers like a teacher. He is very good at qualifying customers to learn which product could be the best choice for them. However, he lacks of closing skills. If customer has objections he does not know enough how to overcome objections. His presentations are boring. He does neither smile nor showing his emotions in his presentations. He is a very good team player and gets along well with everybody in the store. He is not good at retaining old customers as Cathy does. Only approximately 4% of his customers are old customers or referrals.

Tim:

Tim: 1 year sales experience
Total sales up to 1st of June: $290,000
Annual target: $680,000
Gross Margin: %13
Extended Warranty rate: 12%
Average sale: $520, 00
Discount rate: 3%
Closing ratio: %21

Tim:

STRENGTHS	WEAKNESSES
Job commitment	Work-life balance
Warranty sales	Accountability
Motivation, hunger and passion	Appearance
Curiosity	Time management

Scarcity	Mental problems
Presentation	Resiliency
Upselling, cross-selling	Overcoming price objections
Competitiveness	Discounts
Professionalism	Building rapport
Personal development	Team player
Product knowledge	Personal development

Tim:

Tim is an inexperienced salesperson comparing with Cathy and Jason. Although he has never worked in sales and he does pretty well.

He is 42 years old salesman and has four kids. His wife does not work so he is the sole income in his home. Since he has financial problems, he motivates himself to make more money. He has hunger and passion in his job. He believes in what he sells and explains the products with passion in his presentations.

He is eager to learning and developing himself. When he is not with customers, he always tries to learn new tricks and improving his product knowledge. He is good at upselling, cross-selling and selling extended warranties. He got a lot of tricks to do in cross-selling and in upselling.

He knows that upselling and cross-selling are good for his numbers and for his pocket.

For example, when he sells a mattress, he does try to cross-selling everything that are complement to mattress such as pillows, mattress protector, bed frame, duvet set etc. While Cathy and Jason only try to sell mattress protector.

He also compares his sales metrics with his peers to see how he can do better than in areas he needs to improve him and beat other salespeople. He has also curiosity, when he does not know something; he goes to internet or asks his friends to learn. Although he has very good traits, he has also many weaknesses.

He is very slow comparing with other salespeople. If they close a sale in 15 minutes, he finishes a sale almost double more time than them. He is not also good at using cash register. It takes double more time for him to process a sale comparing with others.

He is not also accountable and not honest. He was

caught several times scooping his friends' sales. He lies under pressure to his customers and his co-workers.

He does not have a good personal appearance and he wears the same dress shirt over and over again without washing. He also does not take shower daily and he smells.

He lacks of professionalism. He has strange behaviours like eating hamburgers when customers in the store or he runs in the store like horse when customers in or he yells to other salespeople to ask something. Lastly, he cannot balance his work life with his family life. He brings his home problems to work as Jason does. He also was caught saying customers that he has four kids, his wife does not work. He has to make money to feed his family and he shows his emotions when customer rejects to buy. He has also some sort of mental problems that affect his performance and making him a subject to be gossiped behind. Cathy rumours, gossips and complains a lot behind him and telling him to take his mental pills.

Jennifer:

Jennifer: 5 months sales experience
Total sales up to 1st of June: $260,000

Annual target: $680,000
Gross Margin: %15
Extended Warranty rate: 10%
Average sale: $490, 00
Discount rate: 3%
Closing Ratio: %23

Jennifer

STRENGTHS	WEAKNESSES
Likability	Listening
Appearance	Accountability
Social validation	Job commitment
Warranty sales	Gossiping, chatterbox
Product knowledge	Presentation
Humour in sales	Personal development
Discounts	Unorganized
Resiliency	Work-life balance
Knows about competition	Time management
Overcoming objections	Scarcity

Building relationship	Motivation, passion, hunger
Team player	Lying

Jennifer:

Jennifer worked at competition before coming to this store. Since she has sales experience, she knows a lot about the products. She is the only sales person who uses humour in her sales. She personalizes with customers as Cathy does. She has great networking skills. She always calls her existing customers to follow up with them. She is as good as Tim at warranty sales and she is the best sales person at closing techniques in the store and knows more than anyone how to overcome objections. Although being a personable sales person, she talks to customers about her private life too much.

She is very chatterbox person and does not know when to stop talking. She has some family problems with his boyfriend as Tim and Jason have with their wives.

Her partner does not work so she is the sole income at home. Being sole income at home does not motivate her as Tim does. She has 3 kids and lives far from the store.

She calls sick a lot. She has called sick 8 times in 6 months because she had to take care of her kids. She lacks in sales ethics. She once lied to customer if they buy warranty, the extended warranty covers power surge but actually it did not. She pretended that she did not know about that.

Let's summarize four of these sales people's strengths:

Cathy:

- Cathy is top writer in the store

- She is very personable salesperson with her customers.

- She is the best person about product knowledge in mattresses and she sells more mattress than anyone.

- She has a lot of referrals.

Jason:

- He is the best salesperson in the store in electronics and appliances product knowledge.

- He is a very good team player and get along well with everybody in the store.

- He is very good at qualifying customers to learn which product could be the best choice for them.

Tim:

- He is self-motivated salesperson. He motivates himself to make more money.

    - He is eager to learning and developing himself. When he is not with customer, he reads about sales techniques and product.

    - He is great at upselling and selling warranties. When he sells a product, he got a lot of tricks to upsell accessories.

    - He also compares his sales metrics with his peers to see what he can do be better than them

Jennifer:

- She is the only sales person who uses humour in her sales.

- She has great networking skills.

- *She is the best sales person at closing techniques in the store and knows more than anyone how to overcome objections.

- She is as good as Tim at warranty sales.

Cathy, Jason, Tim and Jennifer are unique in their own way in their sales and in their personal traits. Some of them have the same traits with each other.

Now, I will give you sample pitches of these 4 sales people whose pitches different from each other. Four of them is supposedly going to sell mattress to a lady about 55 years old. She is an accountant and lives on her own.

Let's start with Cathy:

- Cathy: Hello, welcome to our store. What a nice weather we are having today.

- Customer: Yes, it is so nice today but the nicer part is that I am off today.

- Cathy: Lucky you. I am not lucky. When I am off, it is always cold and she smiles. What takes you in today to sacrifice your day-off?

- Customer: Well, I think it is time to change my mattress. My mattress is 12 years old.

- Cathy: Well, I will make your day-off worth. Both smiles.

- Cathy: I think I seen you somewhere. You look very familiar to me. Where do you work?

- Customer: I work at liquor store by Walmart.

- Cathy: Oh yes, now I recognize you. I sometimes go there. Then I saw you there. Do you know Jessica?

- Customer: Of course, she is my manager. I just was with her for a coffee last night.

- Cathy: She is my regular customer. I have sold her a lot of stuff.

They continue chatting about 5 minutes about different things. Cathy asked her questions to qualify her. What size? Do you prefer soft or firm mattresses? Pillow top or not pillow top etc. After narrowed down her choices, Cathy shows her two mattresses and she saw that customer is more interested in the first mattress than the second one she showed her. She continues:

- Cathy: This is the best seller mattress here. I sold it two weeks ago to a lady and she loves it. She came to buy a carpet from me and she said this is the best mattress for her in her life. She used to sink on her mattress too but now, she has a comfy sleep.

- Customer: Let's go for this one then.

- Cathy: I am happy with your decision. I forgot showing you mattress pad and pillow for it.

- Customer: Don't bother about both. I got an awesome pillow and water proof mattress pad.

- Cathy: That's fine then. Let's go to till and finish the process. She finishes the sale, tells her when her mattress will be ready for pick up, shakes her hands, and customer leaves.

Jason:

Now, let's see Jason's pitch shortly. Jason greeted customer, showed her two mattresses like Cathy.

Customer is lying down on mattress. Jason is explaining features of the mattress. He does not have any smile, or emotions. He is too serious with customer. She says I like this one. Let's go for this one.

Jason: That's great. We got mattress pad for it and pillow.

Customer: Oh thank you. I got a great pillow and I will buy a cheap mattress pad at Wal-Mart.

Jason: Okie then, let's go to till and finish the process. She pays; Jason explains when the mattress will be here to pick up. He shakes her hand and she leaves.

Tim:

Tim greeted customer, qualified her with questions to show her the mattresses.

He already showed customer 5 firm mattresses. He asked customer after showing 5 mattresses. What do you like the most?

- Customer: Well, I liked this one and third one the best. They are cheaper too.

- Tim: Let's go to check third one again. They go to third one again and she lies down again. Tim again tells features and benefits about the mattress. He can see that customer seems going to buy this mattress. He thinks it is right time to plant seeds to sell pillow and matt pad.

- Tim: This mattress has 10 years warranty and it covers everything except physical damage and water spill.

Some people sweat and their sweat pour into mattress. Even if you do not sweat, when we sleep with open mouth, water from our mouth goes into mattress, it causes smell, and colour change. Even if you have small spill on your mattress, manufacturer will not honour its warranty. It is their rule.

- Customer: I did not know about that. It is good to know.

- Tim: Buying a mattress without mattress pad like this one is like that buying a brand new car with used tires. Also, this mattress pad wicks away heat to keep you cooler and make you sleep more restful. Also, this pillow has the same technology like mattress pad. It is for side sleepers since you told me you are side sleeper. You wear running shoes when you run, you wear winter boots when it snows and you wear dress shoes when you go to wedding. Having right pillow is the same too. Some people sleep back, some are side sleepers and some stomach sleeper. To have a restful sleep, definitely I would get this pillow as most of mattress customers buy.

- Customer: How much pillow and Matt pad?

- Tim: Pillow is $99,99and matt pad is 119.99

- Customer: They are too expensive. I cannot afford to pay now. I will come back when I have enough money.

- Tim: Tim has heard it all before so he wants to get commitment from customer.

- Well, what I will do for you now that both are on sale and we got limited quantities. Actually, we got only two pillows and three matt pad left but I will give you a good deal. If you pay 10% of total price, we will lock the price for you and if you pay 50%of the price, we will reserve both for you so I can make sure that you will have both them when you pay the rest.

- Customer: Let's pay 50% now.

- Tim: Great idea.

- They finish the payment, he tells the same things like Cathy and Jason and customer leaves without shaking in his hand because he does not shake hands most of the time.

Jennifer:

Now, let's check Jennifer. I will focus on how she gets

away with discount objections.

Let's supposed that customer chose a mattress and she is having price objections about mattress protector and pillow. Jennifer did better job than Tim about explaining features and benefits of mattress protector and pillow. Customer is very obstinate to pay $300 extra to buy mattress protector and pillow ($149, 99 mattress protector and $149,99 pillow).

Customer: I planned to spend $1000 on mattress including taxes. I cannot afford $300.00 more. They are expensive for me. Wal-Mart sells them cheaper. I am passing over both for now.

Jennifer: I understand you darling. I love Wal-Mart too. They sell good stuff too. I like their pie cakes. Well, they make me fatter but they are delicious. She smiles and customer smiles. She says to customer. I wish I had fit body like you. Customer smiles and says, maybe you should stop eating cakes from Wal-Mart. Jennifer starts to call her with name. Well, Britney, It is hard for me to control myself especially when I see my kids eating sweet stuff.

They sell delicious cakes but I am sure that they do not

sell this brand. I was at Wal-Mart last month checking what they were selling. They did not have any moisture wicking technology mattress protectors and pillows.

This brand is only exclusively sold here in the town. It is not really expensive when you consider benefits of the pillow and mattress protector. You pay $300 extra. It could be big amount on you but the mattress protector and pillow comes with 10 years warranty. If something happens to your mattress like sinking, the first thing they check if you have any spill on your mattress. If you have even a small stain on your mattress, the mattress manufacturer will not cover the warranty. Plus, you will have 10 years warranty on mattress protector and pillow. Paying $300 is equal to. $19 cents a day for both considering their lifetime is 10 years ($300\3650days). What's $19 cents? It is not really a lot of money considering how pillow and mattress protector will give you a better sleep without worrying sweating and stains.

You use your pillow and your mattress more than anything in your life.

- Jennifer: How many hours do you sleep Britney?
- Customer: 6-7 hours and 9 hours at weekends.

- Jennifer: Lucky you, my kids make all kind of noise and wake me up when I am off. She smiles. You do not sit constantly 7 hours, you do not drive 7 hours daily, you do not walk 7 hours daily but you sleep 7 hours a daily. So having this mattress protectors and pillow will have you wake up with a restful sleep. We cannot cheat sleeping. So good sleep for a good day is important for us.

- Customer: I agree. I think you are right. Let's go for it.

- Jennifer: Cool, you will not be regretful for this decision.

- They go to cash register and finish the process, she shakes her hands, gives her mattress protector and pillow and let her come next Wed to pick up mattress.

Summary:

If you were a new sales person with no sales experience, who would you want to shadow? Or according to you, who is the best salesperson in the tables?If you asked me this question, I would say I would like to job shadowing four of these personalities in my training. Cathy or Jennifer may be chameleons but they have many shortcomings. Jason is not a definitely chameleon but he has some great positive sides to learn. Tim may or not be considered a chameleon but he has awesome skills to sell warranty. It is the same in our lives. Everybody has some qualities that separate them in a good way; also everybody has some bad traits that separate them in a bad way. These four sales people are truly one of a kind. When we make pizza, we choose what toppings we will put on our pizza.

We can use these four people's strengths as we choose toppings for our pizza and get only what we want to get from them: their strengths.

* Cathy would not probably the best person to learn how to sell extended warranties but she would be a great learning tool for you to learn about how her customers keep coming and buying from her.

* Jason would be a great learning tool for you to learn about TVs and appliances but he would not be a good person to learn about at upselling and cross selling.

* Tim would be a great learning tool for you to learn about warranty sales but he would not be a good example for you about time management.

* Even Jennifer with 6 months experience have some strengths that none of the remaining three do not have. You could learn how she uses humour in her sales but you could exclude her negative traits like being chatterbox.

I have not seen any retail company that allows new salespeople job shadowing different salespeople. They only allow new sales trainees job shadow one person which I think a totally wrong approach. I had given you an example about Ronaldo at earlier pages. Ronaldo learnt different tricks from different players. Job shadowing different salespeople can contribute new trainees to learn tricks of each salesperson as Ronaldo did. Do you think that who would teach you better to sell warranties? Cathy or Tim? Of course Tim, he is good at that even if Cathy is top writer and more experienced salesperson than Tim.

Now, here is the hard part. Most of retail companies are not open to change. They like their way with old fashion. They only allow you don shadow one salesperson.

If they don't allow you shadow different salespeople in your training, then you can at least ask your manager to shadow different salespeople for a few times to see what they do differently from each other.

In the same time, you can ask your friends if they can role play with you in your free times to grab their strengths.

For example, you can ask Jennifer and Tim how they sell warranty or ask Tim what motivates him. Ask Jason if he can do a sample pitch for him in TV sales or appliance sales.

You would not want to miss how Cathy builds a personalized relationship with her customers nor would want to miss Jennifer's humour in her sales nor you not want to miss Tim's motivation and hunger to make money and to be number one. Watch, see, listen, and write down their important tricks.

After you have all of their tricks in your pocket, take them out from your pocket, and blend all of them into your sales.

It is like making a pizza. You have all ingredients of four salespeople to make a pizza along with yours and you got a bowl. Put them into bowl along yours and apply all of their strengths with yours. Don't underestimate the salespeople who are not top writer like Tim or Jennifer. They got definitely some other different strengths that Cathy does not have. As you see, all of these salespeople are unique. Their backgrounds, natural talents, personalities, sales techniques, intellectual levels, their strengths and weaknesses are all different.

We can always learn from others. It does not matter even if they are the worst salesperson. Even the worst salesperson may have something better than the best salesperson to teach you.

Chapter 10: Why Is Role Playing So Important In Sales?

Role play is a valuable and effective training tool that was developed by an Austrian psychiatrist named Jacob Moreno in 1920s. He found out that patients got better so much faster with role plays. Patients acted out their emotions in a psychodrama scene by reacting to each other that that made them feel better.

Role play is a widely used training method used in militaries, in emergency response groups and in some companies. Some of the companies like airlines uses role play method in their simulator training for their pilots to gain ability before they start to fly in actual planes. Role play has been a common training method among military branches, emergency response groups, and companies where quick decision-making is highly valued. So why not to use it in the world of sales training?

How can salespeople benefit from role plays?

Role play has started to be incorporated in business trainings more than before. Companies have started to see the benefits of role plays in their sales trainings. However, the most of retail companies or sales oriented companies still don't use role play technique in trainings. Probably, your company will be one of them. I have worked at variety sectors as sales manager, and as salesperson including insurance, electronics, furniture etc. None of them had role play in their trainings except one company. This company was a furniture company and I can definitely say that their training was the best among the companies I have worked for. Not only they had role play in their training but also they had continuous role play trainings every morning before opening the store for 10 minutes.

Every morning before opening the store, they had one subject to do role play and it was changing every day. In addition that if the store was having problems in certain areas such as warranty sales, drops in margins, or in sales numbers, they used to do role plays by focusing on these subjects.

I will give you a sample schedule for their plays:

Monday	Greetings
Tuesday	How to do presentation
Wednesday	How to create scarcity

Thursday	Overcoming objections
Friday	Cross-selling
Saturday	How to sell mattresses
Sunday	How to sell extended warranty

As I mentioned you that role play subjects used to change weekly except greetings. They used to give importance heavily on greetings and they had greeting role play once a week regardless.

All employees had to join these morning role play sessions without exception. Their role plays were so effective and beneficial for the salespeople. I remember that warranty sales dropped by almost half one time.

They did role play three days on row about warranty sales. The next week, the warranty rates went up by 4% from 7% to 11%. Now, you may ask me that we don't have role play in our company trainings or in our continual trainings on the floor. Then, what can I do?

Firstly, you need to know what your weaknesses are in your sales. If you lack of warranty sales, then find a best salesperson who is the best in warranty sales in your store to and ask him to have role play with him in warranty sales.

He will probably like that because it will boost his ego when you ask him by saying that you are the best in warranty sales so I would like to have your tricks.

Don't be shy. Sell yourself to even to your co-workers to learn something. Any extra knowledge you attain will return you as extra money in your pocket. I had a co-worker who knew everything about TVs. She was so smart. She even knew how many components they used to manufacture a specific TV. I hated TV sales because it was so technical for me. Since I hated it, I had problems to sell extended warranty when I sold TVs. I had difficulties to answer customers' questions that were putting my credibility down. I went to Tim Hortons and picked a double double coffee for my friend for her without telling him. I sat down next to him and put the coffee on front of him. She liked what I did for her. I told her my situation and he said sure I can help you sell warranty on TVs. We did role play for two weeks when we had free times at work. We also did role play on selling TV accessories. Do you know what happened in third week? Sure, my warranty rates went up by 60% and I started to beat him after the fourth week until I quitted the job.

In another example, I had difficulties in dealing with frustrated customers. I used to take their frustrations personally, and arguing with them. I had a customer that who swore at me because her product did not come on time. Well, I started to argue with her which caused more trouble. She left and my manager told me that it is fine that nobody has rights to swear at you. The next day, I talked to our customer service rep in the main cash register if she can help me how to deal with these types of customers. She said of course I can help you Eco. She was very professional person dealing with angry customers and she got used to hearing "f" words a lot. I wrote different angry customer scenarios and used real examples from other sales people or other customer service representatives. We did role playing about a month, I also read how to deal with those customers. It did work. I never had any argument with any customer and they never became rude to me after I learnt how to deal with them with frequent role plays

Summary:

Role play is more than just a form of training. Role plays will help you deal with real problems and help you improve your sales skills. If it was a bad training method, the armies and emergency response units around the world would not use it continually to train their soldiers and their emergency response workers. Any extra information and any extra card to show your customers will come back to you as money.

Chapter 11: The Topics You Should Never Share or Discuss With Your Co-workers

The excess of information can harm you in many situations at work. Sharing personal information about yourself to others may expose your vulnerability to them and may diminish your authority. It can also question your boss whether you are right candidate for promotion.

For example, I had a saleslady who wanted to a sales manager but not promoted because she had too many family problems and used to share all of her family problems with co-workers.

I compiled some of the important things that you should never with your co-workers:

1: Don't reveal too much about your life to co-workers: You probably spend more time with your co-workers than your family. But you should never talk about your personal life with everyone. You must very selective about co-workers with whom you share your family life. Not everyone is trustworthy. If you share your family problems with everyone then you can be subject to having gossips behind you. I had a co-worker who had major problems with his wife. He used to share almost everything with co-workers and they used to gossip behind him. I had another one who was cheating on his wife and used to tell his encounters to some "trustworthy" co-workers. But those "trustworthy" co-workers used to tell everybody what he was doing. You should not also share your intimate details. Sharing your intimate details is excess information. It also will deteriorate your professional image.

2:Don't share information about your earnings:

Telling your co-workers how much you make or how much you sold today can cause resentments and conflicts between you and them. In commission jobs, there is always competition and they are your competition. Revealing too much information about your income can seriously cause jealousy. Jealous co-workers, who know you are better than them in sales, can use this excess information against you in any condition and may try to hit you with the excess information you have provided them. Try to not share your commission earnings or try not brag yourself by saying I made this much and that much today. If they asked you how much money you made today, don't reveal any number. I just made some money. That's it. Keep it simple.

3: Your medical history:

Avoid telling everybody what kind of medical problems you have. Co-workers do not need to know what type of medical problems you have. I had a salesperson who was on depression pills. He used to reveal too much information about his medical situation and others used to love gossiping behind him. Talking about your medical history can create uncomfortable situations at work place for you and for your co-workers. Nobody has to know your medical problems.

4: Don't complain about your work, your working conditions and about co-workers along with your boss:

Revealing to your co-workers your negative experiences regarding with your company, your working conditions, your co-workers and your boss are not a definitely a good idea. Keep your negative experiences for yourself or talk to your manager how you feel.

5. Don't share your personal purchases:

I had salespeople who used to love talking about their personal purchases like fancy cars or jewellery. Your co-workers can get jealous and can blame for you that you make all the money but they don't.

6. Don't talk about politics and religion.

You should avoid discussing these two controversial issues. They usually end with arguments. Everyone has their beliefs and opinions about both. For example, I had a lady who accused a sales person being too religious after they started to talk about the religion. She was disciplined for her actions in the end.

7. Do not reveal information about any of your previous customers:

You must handle your customers' information in discrete. Your co-workers don't have to know how much your customers make nor their job.I had a salesperson who sold stuff to a millionaire and he told about his wealth to everybody at work. When the millionaire person used to come to store to shop, all of the salespeople were racing towards him to greet him!

8. Don't tell anyone that you are looking for another job:

Telling your co-workers that you are looking for another job can discourage them on you and your boss. It may give them the sense that you are not part of the team anymore.

9. Do not share the details of your ideas and plans:

If you have an idea or strategic plans to increase your sales, don't disclose them to your co-workers. Some of them can copy your plan.

10. Don't talk about negative about other races:

Talking about other races is very critical line. You may not like a certain race but you should never talk bad things about other races. I had co-worker who said something very negative about a certain race. Another co-worker jumped into conservation angrily because his mother was from that race. The guy was fired after his racist comments.

Summary:

You can of course talk about positive events and things you have in your life. I don't mean that you should never talk to your co-workers. You are salesperson and you love talking. So you can talk about sports, your physical activities like gym, your and their interests in certain areas etc. You should not cross the line about your sharing. You may share some stuff that you should not and it can aggravate envy and may awaken the negative feelings among your co-workers towards you. You are not salaried person. You work for commission and they are also your competition. Don't give a bullet on their hands to use toward you in the future.

Chapter 12: How to Deal With Negative and Toxic Co-workers?

"Toxic people spread their toxin to you and then you, in turn, become a wasteland like they are." – Body Focus

Negativity hits directly the productivity of salespeople. It is one of the biggest enemies in the sales. When there is negativity at work, salespeople lose focusing on their goal. It is usually accompanied by an atmosphere of gossip, jealousy and family problems. A negative work environment contributes to a boring work environment and this boring work environment results in demotivation, discouragement and significantly cause talent loss. I have dealt with large number of negative salespeople in my career. Especially in a place where I worked was an exceptionally destructive negative place with filled toxic negative employees.

In order you to understand better negativity at a typical sales floor; I made a table for you below:

Celine	Complainer, gossiper
James	Family problems, resilience
Tucker	Mental problems, Family problem, dishonesty
Jamie	Family problems, gossiper
Nora	Family problems, rudeness
Camilla	Family problems
Jaden	Mental problems

Wagner	Anger problems, complainer
Brett	Perfect employee
Eric	Anti-social
Justin	Perfect employee

As you see from the table, 9 out of 11 employees had some sort of problems and were spreading negativity to each other and this negativity was causing toxic and more stress among the employees. I compiled some of their problems in below for you to understand deeply.

Celine: She was working there for 4 years. She used to complain all the time without stopping. She was complaining about the company, about working hours and other employees. She also had major problems with Nora and Tucker. Tucker was written off because of her twice and she was written off once because of Tucker because she said something unacceptable about Tucker's mental health. She also was jealous of Tucker because Tucker started to beat her up in sales in three months.

She also had major problems with Nora. They hated each other. Nora was her store manager so she had power to discipline her. Celine used to love talking negative behind Nora.

James: James did not have any problem with any employees. He was not a resilient salesperson and he had family problems that he used to bring to work and sharing with other salespeople. His wife was about to divorce him because he also used to bring work problems to home. If he could not close a sale, he used to talk over and over why he could not close it and was trying to blame something else. He was also so jealous of other salespeople. He was thinking that other salespeople lie to customers to sell. He was really bad salesperson. He was simply an order taker.

Tucker: Tucker was a friendly salesperson. He was in his world and he was trying to be best. Money was a main motivator for him to be the best salesperson. Celine hated Tucker. She was that Tucker was a threat to her in sales. Tucker was 42 years old gentleman with four kids but he was scared by Celine. He was even looking for another job because of her bad behaviour to him. He was also on mental pills. He had learning disability and was forgetting quickly and his emotions used to chance a lot. His wife also was treating him bad at home and she even slapped him several times. One-day, I saw him that he was hugging his wife on the centre at the store. I thought that something good happened because they were smiling. I asked him after his wife left: what did happen Tucker? Why were you hugging her? He said: I had forgotten bringing my depression pills. She brought me them so I wanted to hug her. He was making too many mistakes in his sales and he was too slow with his sales because of his mental problems. Overall, he was a team player and he was a nice guy.

Jamie: She had family problems like James and Tucker. She had three kids from three different men and she was pregnant her fourth child from another man. Her boyfriend did not work and they had fights at home. She used to love talking about every fight she does with her boyfriend and was sharing those fights with salespeople at work. She also loved gossiping behind others. She hated Tucker and Nora. She loved talking negative behind them.

Nora: She was store manager. She was very rude to customers. She was complainer to the head office too many times by customers. In one instance, one of my customers called her a bitch. In another instance, a customer harassed her badly because she was rude to her. The most interestingly, when I worked at the competition before, I had customers who drove to us to buy furniture because she was known as rude in the town. Her boyfriend had alcohol problems and it was affecting her work balance. He used to get drunk almost every night and they were fighting almost every night. Her parents wanted to her divorce but she was religious. According to her belief, divorcing was a sin. She was also also trying to have a child but she had infertility issues. She spent over $50,000 to have a baby but failed.

Camilla: Camilla was overall a good employee. She had very minor family issues comparing others. She burst into tears when the customers were in the store because her bf dumped him. It was not very professional behaviour to burst into tears among the customers.

Jaden: This guy was the best friend of Nora's husband. They used to hang out together and got drunk. He was on cocaine also. He had suicidal thoughts and had terrible fights with his girlfriend. He was so lazy and not was doing his job properly. Everybody knew that he was so lazy including Nora who hired him because he was the best friend of his husband.

In one instance, he came to work late and told me that he was almost killing himself last night after fighting with his girlfriend by crying. This is the guy was paying 25% interest monthly to buy a car because he had bad credit score.

Wagner: Wagner was very hard worker. He did his tasks

without asking him. However, he was antisocial person. He hated Jaden and Nora. He attempted to hit Jaden once and he also used to have major fights with Nora. In one fight with her, he used to call her with the worst vulgar words you can imagine. He also threatened Tucker and Derrick but he got away with that. He was always in negative mood about the work. He hated working there but it was harder for him to find a job. He was trying to find another job.

Brett: He was a great employee with no problems. Unfortunately, he was a part time worker.

Eric: He was overall good person with others except Wagner. They were working together. Wagner hated him. He was antisocial person. He barely used to talk others and he was so serious person like Sylvester Stallone.

Justin: He was another part time employee like Brett. He was a wonderful person with a positive attitude.

Let's see what we can do prevent arguments with these types of employees:

1. Try to not argue with them:

Never try to argue with them, it will be impossible to win. They will never admit their mistakes and when they make mistakes, they will blame something else. They have generally very strong opinions and they will never change that whatever you tell them. They will find and create many reasons to back up themselves. Arguing with them will demoralize you in the end.

2. Empathize with them:

You probably had a bad day and someone approached to you and cooled you down by saying something positive. I know how you feel but just look on the bright side. I'm sorry you are going through this. Thank you for sharing with me etc. and try to change the subject.

3. Try to change the subject:

If your co-worker is having a family problem at home all the time, then it is hard to change his negative attitude. No matter what you say to him, he will be the same next day. Try to bring a new theme to improve his mood. Things he likes to do, talking about common friends etc. Talk about the areas he likes.

4. Try to ignore:

If they are negative, pretend you are listening to them. Also, pretend that you agree with them and find an excuse to leave. I am sorry I forgot doing my errands or something else.

5. Ask them help:

If they do something better than you in sales, ask them how you can improve yourself and be like them. They feel great when you tell that to them. In addition that acknowledge their success (if they have any). They like if you tell them that you did very good last month in sales or something else related with their sales.

6. Give them compliments:

These toxic people love having praised. Say something, where did you get your shoes? They look wonderful on you. Which hair dressers do you go for your hair? Your hair looks superb on you. They will suddenly stop being negative. That does work. Try it. You are going to see how they become happy right away and talk about themselves with a positive attitude.

7. Control your reactions and change perceptions:

You can try to change your perceptions about handling negativity. Try to focus on seeing good sides of that person. Try to interpret their negativity with positivism. I know it can be hard at first but this does work too.

8. Be formal with them:

This is the most crucial part with dealing these people. You will have dilemma. If you completely avoid them, you work with 8 hours shift with them and it is going to be very difficult to see them all around you. Instead of avoiding them completely, be formal with them and keep your relation with them in distance.

Summary: Wherever you work, there will be some type of these people. We cannot change the jobs because of them but we can learn how to handle them. Complaining about them will not solve the problem either. A person is negative when throughout the day their only comments were of that tone. A negative person loves to complain about the work, workmates, their boss, their company, their customers, their products, their price etc. Nothing will satisfy these types of people whatever you do. They will always find something to complain about. Negative people will be part of our lives. Escaping from them by quitting your job is not a solution. I know that you are not a psychiatrist but we need to be a psychology in sales not only for them but also customers. Here is another opportunity for you to make: dealing with these types of toxic employees will also help you dealing with rude customers or dealing with difficult customer experiences.

"Don't destroy yourself by allowing negative people add gibberish and debris to your character, reputation, and aspirations. Keep all dreams alive but discreet, so that those with unhealthy tongues won't have any other option than to infest themselves with their own." diseases."-Michael Bassey Johnson

Chapter 13: How to be Resilient and How to be Overcome Customer Rejections?

> *"What helps you persevere is your resilience and commitment."-Roy T. Bennett*
>
> *"A rejection is nothing more than a necessary step in the pursuit of success."-BoBennett*

As a professional salesperson, you will often experience rejection by your customers. Having rejected is by customers is simple a part of salespeople. As time goes on, you will try to strengthen yourself to cope with the rejections by the customers. If you cannot strengthen yourself with customer rejections, and if you cannot skip the rejections in your mind, then it will affect your next sale and your day at work. It is not all bad that your customer rejected you. You can analyze and identify reasons behind the "no "and take advantage of these no's to improve yourself.

Study on rejections:

Write down why you were rejected and develop techniques and game plans to reduce rejections. Was it time, your presentation, your competition, your attitude or something else? Write down and work on them. For example, if your customer did not buy because he wanted to check the prices in your competition, then write down, learn from your co-workers, learn from your sales manager, study about your competition to overcome competition objections.

Use rejections as opportunity to get better:

You can use the rejections as opportunity to get better .For example, one of the bad salespeople I worked with pointed out a chair with his fingers from 70 feet away when customer asked him he was looking for the chair he saw in the website.Customer went to see the chair and the salesperson approached the customer 2 minutes later. Customer took his pointing out style as offensive. He did not buy the chair from him but from another salesperson. He never did that again.

Be strong emotionally:

Top salespeople manage the rejections more effectively from. They think that the rejections are like roller coaster and never stop. One day you are up and the next down. They see it is part of their job.

Think logical:

Not every customer enters in your store to purchase. In fact, average closing ratio in retail stores is 20% to %30. In average, only 2.5 customers buy out of 10 customers.

Don't take them personal: Not each customer is ready to buy your products in that given day. When you are rejected, you must keep a positive attitude and focus on moving on to next sale. Understand that rejection is not directed at you personally. It can come from various reasons: Bad experience from previous salesperson, prices, timing etc.

Learn from co-workers:

Get help from your sales manager or from experienced salespeople how to handle customer rejections. Learn their tricks how to move on from a rejection.

Don't waste your time with negative thoughts:

Don't brag your co-workers or make your mood negative because customers did not buy from you. Be positive. There will be good days too. Having a positive mindset and having psychologically strong mindset is important for your next sales pitch.

Rejections are not a fail:

You have to know that having rejections are not a fail but a step towards success. If you use rejections to motivate yourself, you can have success in your sale career as how Michal Jordan and Beatles did. Michael Jordan was rejected by his high school team; he went to home and cried. Later, he thought that crying was not a good solution. He motivated himself to be the best. When they were very young, Beatles was rejected by a recording company but they did not give up being the best.

Summary:

Rejection by customers may hurt us like physical pain. It may demoralize us when we think back to that moment. It has the same effect as we were punched out in our face. With a positive thinking and motivation we can overcome it luckily.

I had a salesperson that made a sad face impression to her customers when she lost selling three expensive computers with warranty. Customer tried to console her by saying: Don't worry Britney, we will come back and buy from you. Don't be like her. There are always nexts in the sales. You must always move on next sale without thinking previous bad sale. There is a good saying: To keep balancing, you keep pedalling on the bike. If you cannot continue pedalling, then you will not have full performance and confidence to close your customer and you will ruin your day and maybe your sales career. Having knowing how to respond negative situations by being resilient will increase your speed of recovery. You must know how to bounce back regardless of situations and keep your positivism. Be resilient and have tenacity!

Chapter 14: Important Personal Traits to be Successful

I compiled some of important personal traits that you should have in sales. I mentioned and will mention some of other important traits like resiliency in the previous pages. Let's check what these important traits to have:

1. Be organized
2. Be an opportunity creator
3. Curiosity
4. Honesty
5. Don't be shy
6. Compare your numbers with your peers
7. Be sociable:(outgoing, sociable)
8. Don't have discouragement
9. Be modest and be humble
10. Have confidence
11. Have self-motivation

1. **Be organized:**

Unfortunately, many sales people are disorganized. They are hard to admit this reality but it is true. Many forget their client's name, they forget an appointment date, they never follow up with their customers. They do not keep notes, they do not have binders, they do not have copies of the quotes they gave to customers, they forget what their customers were interested when they come back or they are rushing to find their customer's quotes in their binders in unprofessional manner. Show your customers confidence that you are organized and you are right person to buy from them. Instead of using your phone to look at Facebook at work, use your phone for your business and to organize yourself. If you are disorganized, accept that reality and change yourself. Do not find excuses like I am overloaded, I am too busy etc.

2. **Be an opportunity creator:**

"Failure is simply the opportunity to begin again, this time more intelligently"- Henry Ford

Salespeople should be creative, positive and they should always look for opportunities to grasp and convert them into sales. There is an old story about a shoe manufacturer that shows us how thinking of outside the box is important in the sales. A shoe company sent one of his salespeople to an island in the Pacific to investigate if the company could sell their shoes. After a few days, the salesperson sent a message to his manager and said:

- It is impossible to sell shoes here, because everyone walks on barefoot. The manager decided to verify if his salesperson is right, so he sent another salesperson to the island. A few days later, the second salesperson called the company and said:
- There are some opportunities to sell shoes here. The islanders are on barefoot here. The manager is confused between two salespeople's responses, so he decided to send his best salesperson to the island. The best salesperson went to the island, took his time, did some research and called his manager and said:

- People have really bad foot here, and they would benefit wearing shoes and recommended to manager:
- We should design shoes accordingly their needs.
- We should invest in advertising to inform the islanders about the benefits of wearing shoes.
- We should give free samples head of the tribes because if they like our shoes and they have recommend us to the islanders because they have the power of influence and the authority. It would be easier for us to get into the market by getting referrals from the head of the tribes.

As you see that three salespeople had reported the things differently.

- The first salesperson was a bad salesperson. He could not see outside of the box.

- The second salesperson was medium performing salesperson. He understood that they needed shoes but he could not create any opportunity because he could not see outside of the box.

- The last salesperson was a top performer. He was a great example what it takes to be a top salesperson. He was very positive, he took his time, he talked to people and he caught opportunity by pinpointing benefits of wearing shoes and how to market and sell them. You must always think of outside of the box. You can create opportunities by thinking outside of the box.

  For example, you see an old couple coming into your store. You can go to the door and open the door for them or your customers are tired. You can pull the chair and let them sit. Your customers are sweating; you can give them a napkin to clean their face. These are small details for you to be opportunistic. It is also confused that opportunist people use other people. You don't want to be that type of opportunistic person but you want to be opportunistic person who help you customers without using them which means: just selling what they need or may need. I went to Rome in Italy for vacation. I saw an East Asian guy selling umbrellas in a rainy weather at the Nuovo Mercato Esquilino entrance.(Farmers Market). It was pouring down; I did not want to get wet so I bought an umbrella from him before leaving. I went out to see the Colosseum next day. I saw him again close to the Colosseum. He was selling the bottled water. People were standing in the line to get into the Colosseum. It was hot and humid. This time, he was selling bottled water to people who were standing in the line. I bought water from him because nobody was selling water around and I did not want to lose my spot in the line.This guy is a real example of opportunity maker. He knew that people don't visit the Colosseum much in rainy weathers so he was selling umbrellas at farmers market. Not only he created opportunity by using weather but he smartly waited in right places according to weather conditions. Like him, you should always know where to be and how to fall down in all situations. You should know how to create opportunities by thinking smaller details. Opportunities rarely will come to you if you don't know how to think outside of the box and create them. For example, oil was discovered in 1859 in Pennsylvania and the Oil Boom had begun. A young business man John D. Rockefeller saw the opportunities in this new industry. He was intrigued with the future of this industry. He saw that there were a lot of companies drilling the oil but only few companies refine the oil. However, they did not know how to refine the oil efficiently and they were wasting it due to inefficient extraction methods. He saw this problem and wanted to create a opportunity to refine oil efficiently and less expensive. So he and his partners decided to refine the oil instead of drilling it. In 1863, they established the Standard Oil and succeeded to refine oil more efficiently and less costly than others. From the beginning of the end till 1811, they controlled almost all oil industry. As you see that they were opportunity makers. They looked at situations differently to create opportunities unlike other companies.

I will give you another example about creating opportunities: I had a customer who was interested in buying an high-end sofa with wool fabric on it. She had two cats and they were leaving their hair on everything at home. She said it is too difficult to remove their fur. I already had known that wool does not go well with cat fur. I tried to show her alternatives but she did not like alternates. She was only interested in that sofa. Money was not issue for her but she is so scared of cleaning cat fur because it was taking a lot of time for her. I talked to my manager to see if we can do a custom made sofa with the same design but with different fabric. She said we can but it will take three months. I told her that I got great news for you that we can make a custom made sofa for you only in three months. She said I cannot wait three months and shovelled me off. I planned to create an opportunity by offering her a strong vacuum cleaner for pets. I went and grabbed a Dyson Ball Animal Vacuum Cleaner to do a short demonstration on the sofa and on the floor. I told her that this vacuum cleaner can literally get your cat's hair out of everything. It is also great for stairs, ceiling fans. The most importantly, I don't want you to have cat fur on you. It is going to be removing your cat's fur from your clothes. She had some cat fur on her jacket. I changed the accessory in the vacuum cleaner and wiped out the pet hair from her right arms and told her: can you see that how this vacuums cleaner removed the pet hair in five seconds. She loved my demonstration. She said that you are great salesperson. You do not need tell me anything else because I am happy what you did for me to sell your products. She bought both products with extended warranty with three matching pillows for her sofa.

Look for opportunities:

In your sales, everything can be an opportunity for you to turn into sales. You should focus on things that can increase your likability on your customers. You focus on finding a problem and create an opportunity to build a better rapport. For example, your customer said you that it is too hot in the store. Then, you can go to air conditioner and make it cooler. This situation is a problem for them and you can make an opportunity for you to increase your likability by them. (Changing air conditioner temperature may not be allowed at your store so you may ask your manager. If you are not allowed then you can tell the customer). As long as they see your effort, they will appreciate you. You may also ask your customers if it is cold or warm and try to change temperature according to their answer. Try to use this air conditioner option for the customers with who you are having hard time to build rapport. Your efforts will increase your likability.

3. **Curiosity:**

You must have hunger about customers' needs and problems. The more information you can collect, the easier you can close your sale. I go to gym everyday. If a salesperson asked me: what exercises do you do at gym? I would love to talk about my experiences. Being curious about their lives will help you build a personalized rapport with them. Don't forget being a chameleon. A curiosity is one of paths to be a chameleon.

4. **Honesty:**

Be honest with your customers no matter what happens. Don't lie, if you don't lie, then you don't have to remember what you have just said.

5. Don't be shy:

Don't be embarrassed to sell or don't be shy to get a yes from them. You are there to take their money by providing your products. If they say no to buy, round the words get a yes.

6. Compare your numbers with your peers: The competition means more money for you. If you check and compare your numbers with your peers, you can motivate yourself faster to beat them up in sales.

7. Be sociable :(outgoing, sociable)

Be social with them. Behave as if you know them for years. Find common grounds to talk, use humour, make moderate jokes etc.

8. Don't have discouragement:

If you did bad today, it does not mean you will do bad again tomorrow. Don't be discouraged by a bad day, by a bad customer or something negative at your work.

9. Be modest and be humble:

Don't brag how good you are at sales. Be modest with your co-workers and with your customers. If your customer says that you are the best salesperson she dealt with, don't tell her that yes, I know I am the best salesperson; I am the top salesperson in our store etc.

10. Have confidence:

I believe that this is one of the most important personality traits you should have. I am not talking about having confidence on your products. I have sold products that I have not even believed in but I have had confidence about myself. Even if I did not believe in what I had sold, I behaved as if I had been selling the best product. Nobody is born with limitless self-confidence including you. I am not a psychologist but I can tell you one thing sure: you must have confidence on yourself. You must show your customers that you are confident enough to sell them. You must always hold the rope during the sale process and you cannot let your customers hold the rope. I will give more emphasis on confidence in my next book. It is again very important and do have confidence on yourself.

12. Have self-motivation:

I will write a little about motivation since there is much information online for you to find subjects about motivation. As salesperson, you have to motivate yourself. Money is usually top motivator for salespeople. If money is your goal too, then you have to motivate yourself to make money. But motivating yourself to make the most money comes at cost. Motivation alone is a vague term. You have to donate yourself with core sales skills and product knowledge. If you don't know your products, no matter how you motivate yourself, you will not get the result. If you don't know how to build a personalized rapport, no matter what you do, you will not make the money you want to make. Therefore, firstly you must motivate yourself for the areas you lack of the skill, and afterwards money will come along.

Chapter 15: Difference Between Optimist and Positive Sales People

You may think that they are the same but they are not actually the same terms. Optimist salespeople think that the sales will be better for them in the future. They think that something will good happen in the future but they do not involve how good things will happen. They don't involve how their sales will increase or they don't get lessons from the past. Positive salespeople are on the same page as optimist people about thinking of the future but on contrary to optimist salespeople, they directly involve in the future. Not only they think that everything is going to be well but they also work to make their future better with positivism. They also shape the future in accordance with circumstances they can control not the things they cannot control with. I will give you a good example about a positive salesperson. There was a snow storm and our store was so empty. 3 out of 5 salespeople could not come to work due to the storm so there were only two salespeople working. One of them was busy with calling his previous customers to ask if they are all right in the storm. Afterwards, he was inviting them to store next week for VIP sale. He is a great example how you can create positivism from the things you cannot control. This salesperson was the best salesperson in the store that time. Whereas, the other salesperson was busy with playing card games on his phone. When I asked him, how does he feel the store being not busy? He said: well today is one of those days. Once storm is over, they will come back. There is no need to worry about this. I have worked here for 5 years and we have always had snow storms here in winters. His approach was completely different than other salesperson. He is a great example of the optimist salesperson. I asked the positive salesperson: why was he calling his customers today? He said this is a great opportunity to call them to ask them if they were all right in snow storm and with this excuse, I can invite them in our store in VIP sale. He was a smart, opportunistic and a positive salesperson. He did not wait opportunities to come to him but he took steps to create opportunities by thinking positive.

Chapter 16: Paradox of Choice

"Too many choices can overwhelm us and cause us to not choose at all. For businesses, this means that if they offer us too many choices, we may not buy anything."- Sheena Iyengar

"Too much choice kills the choice". As saying says showing your customers too many options confuse them. Not only showing too many choices to your customers increase your time, and your effort to sell but also it increases their time to gather information and to make a decision. According to psychologist Barry Schwartz from Swarthmore College:" As the number of options increases, the costs, in time and effort, of gathering the information needed to make a good choice also increase,". He also says: "The level of certainty people have about their choice decreases. And the anticipation that they will regret their choice increases. "A research completed by Sheena S. Iyengar Columbia University, and Mark R. Lepper Stanford University points out that overloading with choices people can delay buying decisions and can generate a negative well-being. They did a research with jams in a leading gourmet store in California. They put two tables side by side. They put only a group of 24 types of jams in first table. They put a group of six type of jams in second table. The table with 24 jams generated more interest than the table with six jams. However the results were astonishing. Only 3 % of people who sampled the table with 24 jams bought while 30% of people who sampled the table with six jams bought. As we see that when there are fewer choices, it helps customers make their decisions faster to buy by reducing complexity. Trader Joe's is a great example offering their customers limited products comparing giant chains like Whole Foods. The company significantly restricts customers' choices. They only offer handful of options for customers to choose from. They are successful at that too. Joe's outperformed competitors like Whole Foods in terms of sales per square footage according to Retail Lease Trac. Joe's sales per square foot was $1723, and Whole Foods only made $937 worth sales for per square foot in 2014.English retailer giant Tesco followed Joe's business principle and decided to reduce approximately 60% of their products from shelves to make their stores less baffling to compete more efficiently with their competitors in 2015. Their competitions like German Aldi only offered 2000-3000 products while Tesla offered 90,000 products. You probably had the paradox of choice dilemma too when you go to supermarket. There are many brands, many types of pizzas for you to choose from but if there were few options, you would make your decision faster to buy. In another example related to us that we like changing channels. We have tendency to zap from channel to channel to find a suitable program for us but the more we zap channels, the more time we spend to find a suitable program for us that makes us undecided and also makes us to lose time while zapping. Most of people like shopping at Amazon. They have tons of choices from different sellers. We go there and check products and read reviews and trying to make a decision to buy. Sometimes, it takes days to choose from. For example, I checked how many Nike men's shoes Amazon sells. They don't show exact quantity but when you search Nike Men's Shoes, they give you over 20,000 options. Just say they got exactly 20,000 shoes. I went to Nike official website; they have only 862 men's shoes.

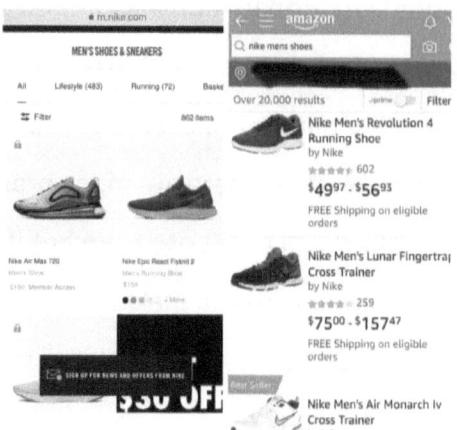

When there are many options to watch, our brain needs more time to decide, and it must review which of them is better for us and many times it will end up reviewing and reviewing to decide. On the other hand, if there are a few channel options to choose from or a few shoes then we would make our decision faster to choose a channel or to buy a pair of shoes.

Do you know what is difference between a commander and a referee?

A referee watches the game and maintains standards of the play and makes binding decisions according to the law of the sport. Meanwhile, the commander directly involves in the actions by commanding his soldiers with his verbal commands. As salesperson, you cannot watch your customers choosing products but you must control and command your sale by showing your option according to their needs. If you watch them like a referee, then you will have major problems. I feel hearing you that you have many products in your store to choose from. I know you cannot prevent your company to display too many products in the store. Every company has different policies and sales strategies to sell their products like Joe's and Whole Foods. One limits the products in the store and the other does not limit. So, you must limit what you will show your customers as Joe's does. Qualifying questions and asking right questions to them will help you reduce the options. For example, if you got a customer comes into your store and asking you that he is looking for a cheap sectional for spare room. He also wants it to be fabric. Then you can start to reduce his options. As you know, people do not want to spend much on furniture for spare rooms and he already mentioned you that he wants something cheap, smaller and it is for spare room. For any customer telling you that they want something cheap, then we would make hardly money. Your job as commander starts here:

Just say, there are 15 sectionals in your store:

12 out of 15 are fabric.

8 out of 12 are small.

2 our out of 8 are over $1000.

6 out of 8 are under $1000

Now you eliminated their choices to 6 sectionals. You should pick a sectional from over $1000 range and pick up two sofas under $1000. You picked a sectional over $1000 range which is sold for $1500. You picked two sectionals under $1000 range: Sectional Daisy and Sectional Tulip. Sectional Daisy is sold for $800 and Sectional Tulip is sold for $600. You got three options to show your customers now. Always start from the most expensive one. He will probably think that it is too expensive but what will you lose by showing the expensive one even if he has asked something cheap. Explain features and benefits the expensive one and watch customer's reactions. Try to create value. If he resists the price then downgrade to him cheaper options. When there are few options are presented, then your customers will make their decision faster to buy. I have dealt with terrible salespeople who took customers from the products to products to show. As salesperson; you must lead the sale with confidence. Showing customers too many products show that you lost your confidence and customers lead and control your sale. You must qualify your customers with right questions to reduce their options.

Do these steps for all products you sell:

- Always start from the most expensive to the least expensive.
- It is easier to downgrade than upgrade.
- Don't lose the control of your sale. Once you lose the control, customers will wander around to see all of the sofas or they will want you to show others. Give them the confidence and credibility about what you sell. You are a salesperson not a clerk in grocery store. I had salesperson that was showing all of the mattresses in the store to his customers. He used to say: I want you to have the best mattress so I want you to try all mattresses we have in our display. Well, we had 14 mattresses in our store. One by one, he was making his customers to lay down in mattresses and explaining benefits and features. It was taking over an hour for to sell a mattress and he also used to lose a lot of sales because he used to make

customers confused with too many options and used to demotivate them to buy because of too many options. He had also highest return percentage in mattresses because customers ended up less satisfied the result of choice. If you want to make money, and if you want to save time in your sales, you should be a commander. You should limit options to your customers according to their needs. You will see that it will boost your sales and your wallet. Showing your customers all of the products mean that you don't have confidence in your sales and you have lost of your control in your sales. Don't steal your and their time, show less and show right products.

Chapter 17: Handling Promotions

Retail companies know that sales promotions one of the most effective methods to increase the sales. Retail sales promotions can be in many different forms. As salesperson, you don't decide what type of promotions your company makes or will make. They deal with that. Promotions are one of the bullets in your arsenal to use when needed to close your sale in right time. Although there are many types of different promotions, I will focus on five of them. I will show you how to use these promotions as a bullet to close your sales and overcome objections.

Let's start with some of important ones:

1: Secret Sales:

Your company may have secret sales. Secret sales usually are not advertised in company website or on flyers or on price tags. They are secret as name says. You can use these secret sales as closing tool and to sell warranty. I did close too many sales thanks to secret sales. Customers don't know which products are on secret sale. They check the price tags and see what are in the price tags.

Let's do a role play to illustrate this better:

You are customer and I am salesperson and I am selling you a fridge. I showed you three fridges after qualifying you with questions and we agreed in one Samsung fridge with price tag $1399.99 but you want to think about it. You want to talk to your wife. I want you to sell the fridge now because you may leave and not come back again. A persistent salesperson in competition may persuade you better than me. I will use the secret sale to close the sale now. In the second example, I will use it to sell the extended warranty.

- I: We agreed that this fridge is the best option for you.

- Customer: Well, I know it is great fridge but it is more than I can afford.

- I: How much is it more expensive than what you initially budgeted?

- Customer: Well, I was looking for a fridge under $1000

- You: Well, I understand that money does not grow on trees. You are a carpenter and my brother is a carpenter like you. He works hard like you. I want to make you save money. I have a great news for you and I have a bad news for you. Which ones would you like to hear first?

- Customer: Tell me the good one.

- I: I forgot you mentioning that we had secret sale. If you buy the fridge today, it is $200 extra off. So lets meet in the middle. After $200 off, total prices drops to only $1199. This deal ends today and you are lucky that we have only a few fridges left in our stock. And the bad news is that I will not see you again till your next purchase. I liked to talk to you.

- Customer: Let's finish this then.

  To sell warranty:

  Customer decided to buy warranty but she things it is expensive for them. You planted the seeds to sell warranty in your presentation and now it is time to sell warranty. 3 years warranty is $299.00

  If you say directly: I will give you off $199.99 off on price tag if you buy the warranty will not be any good and any ethical. Oh my god, I forgot something saying you very important. Actually, this could be the most important thing you heard in your life. (You smile and only use this sentence if you have a personalized rapport).

I will make you save you money. I will give you $199.99 off on the price so you will $199.00 and pay only $99.00 for our favourite and preferred warranty. Customer rejections will decrease and eliminate if you tell the secret sale price to sell warranty. Make sure that you tell the customer that you forgot mentioning you got secret sale price on the fridge and she would get $200 off even if she did not buy warranty. In second example, you use the same tricks. If the price of the fridge is not an objection for the customers, if they already decided to buy it, use your bullet to sell warranty. Pitch your warranty first and see if they have objections in the extended warranty price. If they do, tell them that I have a great news for you. Extended warranty costs $300 for three years and I forgot mentioning you earlier that we have a secret sale in this fridge. It is $200 off on the price tag. So you will only pay $100 for warranty actually. This tactic does work too.

Note: Even if they decide to buy warranty without objections and without know the secret sale, tell them that I forgot mentioning you that we have $200 secret sale on this fridge so it will cost you $200 less. Be ethical and mention and give $200 off even if they are all right with price.

2: One-time exchange guarantee:

Your company may have a trial period up to certain period for mattresses or for some other products. If your customer want to buy a mattress, don't tell your customers right away that they have one time replacement guarantee up to a certain date. (Could be up to 90 days)

Show the mattresses after qualifying your customers, and if they seem that they are undecided to buy or not, if their concern is sleeping quality of the mattress, then it is the time to use your bullet. I do understand that you worry that you may not like it when you have it. Once you buy a brand-new car, will your car dealer accept a one-time free replacement? (Most don't). They will say no. Well, I have great news for you. We have 90 days Satisfaction guarantee. If you don't like your mattress which I don't think because as

I already mentioned you before that I have sold this mattress many times and they love it. But even if your car dealer does not accept onetime free exchange guarantee, we will. If you think that your mattress is not what you expected, bring us after using it 21 days, we will replace it with another mattress once. How is my deal? And sometimes I was using the humour and adding: Well, I think I talked fast with my broken accent with a smile. They always said with no exception: no your accent is fine with smile.

Note: Watch your line here. If you tell your customers that I will do one time exception for you and give up 90 days replacement guarantee, then you will have ethical dilemma. Always do say that our company has 90 days satisfaction guarantee. This technique works mostly with customers who have objections about quality and not price.

3: Giveaways:

Companies give some free products if customers buy a certain period.

For example, if customers buy a mattress, they give free pillows. You can use this promotion to close your sale. Your customer seemed undecided to buy the mattress you showed them. You let them lay down on mattress already. You explained features and benefits. They told you that they like it but meantime they want to think about it. You use free pillow options to close the sale.

Dear customer, how did you like the pillows I gave you to try on the mattress. I have great news for you. I am going to give these two pillows free today when you buy this mattress because they are on promotion. Always use these free giveaways to close the sale not in the beginning of the sale. Always keep some bullets (tricks) in your pocket to use later on. Even if they buy with no objections, still tell them that you forgot that this mattress come with free pillows.

Free Shipping:

If customers spend up to a certain amount, they get free shipping. Again, don't tell right away that they get free shipping if they spend that much, they get free shipping. Only use this promotion to overcome objections.

Summary:

Using promotions in right place and in right time are going to help you close your sales and help you sell warranty. It may have happened to you that you went to a store and wanted to buy a jacket. The price was $199.99 and you liked that jacket. But you think it is expensive. A sales associate comes to you and showing other jackets but you want that jacket. She says the price dropped to $139, 99. We did not have time to change tags. What would you do? I am pretty sure that you would buy it. Be ethical with your customers when you use these promotions to close your sales. Always tell them that I forgot mentioning... when you use them as a bullet. The main customer objection must be price. These tricks can work other objections like time, but they do work better at price objections. If you can structure your presentation effectively, you are not going to have any problem to use these promotions to close your sales. Again, don't start off your product presentation by saying one of those promotions right away at start. Weight, measure and take action accordingly.

Chapter 18: Customer Relations and Customer Dialogues

- Selling couples
- Breaking the ice
- Retaining old customers
- Follow- ups
- Don't badmouth your competition
- Lying to customers
- Dealing with angry customers
- Choosing and judging customers
- Don't leave your customers alone
- Don't hand flyers out your customer
- Use clipboards
- Phone calls
- What not to share with your customers

Selling couples:

When you sell couples, you must make sure that both of them clearly understand you. Sometimes, wife or husband can give you hard time not to buy. Make sure that when you talk to them, look at both of their faces and keep eye contact on both. If you only to talk to one of them, one of them may be offended that happened to one of my co-workers. Wife of a customer complained to store manager because salesperson only looked at her husband, he was not interested in her at all and salesperson only talked to him. Make sure to pay attention to both. You should always try to get both of their approval to sell. Otherwise, it could be another return for you. If there are more people than two, then focus on decision making person more than others.

Breaking the ice:

Some customers don't trust commissioned sales people for different reasons. In addition to those people, some customers want to look at the products on their own. Here are some scenarios about how to break ice with these type customers.

Scenario: Customer just came into your store and you approached customers with a good smile and greeted your customer. Customer suddenly said: I am just looking with a negative face impression. This is the sign that you should leave the customer alone. You may say use humour to see their reactions change or not: Dear customer, you are one of the luckiest people today. We have a promotion today. Whatever you look at, it is free today etc. If you see that customer's reaction changed, then you can continue talking. Otherwise, you should leave them alone for certain period of time. Keep a 15-20 feet distance from your customers and pretend doing something such as cleaning the products in store, or occupying yourself with price tags or pretend writing something on your binder. Meantime watch what your customers do and what type of products they are mostly interested without giving them the impression that you are watching them. After 5-10 min, or when you see they are standing by a certain product and taking their time with only that product, it is your time to go back to your customers and directly tell them something mixed with humour. You can say something like: I like your taste. You found one of the best products in our store. How do you like it? Etc.

Don't say: can I help you back, can I help you? Are you interested in this product? Don't hang behind them as cats chasing toys. Those type customers want to be alone. I went to Adidas store in Istanbul and got a gym pants to try. I went to cabin to try it. The store was not busy. Sales associate followed me to cabin and waited for me. I tried to gym pants and I liked it. But I did not buy it because he was waiting by the cabin like a soldier. I left and bought my gym pants at Nike.

Retaining your old customers:

"Make a customer, not a sale." – Katherine Barchetti

There is an old saying: "Make new friends, but keep the old". According to smallbiztrends, the probabilities to sell old customers are 60-70 % more than selling new customers. According to Marketing Metrics, 34% of customers went to competition to shop because they were dissatisfied with salespeople or service at old company. Don't forget their purchasing history and contact information: You should keep track of each of your customers by keeping their previous invoices in a separate binder at work. I had a friend who had invoices of his customers three years back. You can also use old salespeople's invoices to call their old customers. For example, I used to extract old salespeople's invoices from computer and used to call them. It used to do work. One-day, I called an old customer who had bought three years ago. I introduced myself and I asked them if they had any problems? They said everything is fine and it was nice to hear to remember us after three years. She said we need a king size mattress and laundry set. I invited them to store and closed a $6,000 sale. I closed many sales thanks old customers and you can do too! You got nothing to lose but something to win if you try! Retaining your old customers and keeping them for life is easier than selling new customers as you see in my example above. Whenever you close a sale, ask your customers their email address, their phone number and where they live. If they think of buying something else in the future, take that product name as note in your binder too. Ask them if you can mention their name to your customers as reference. If you provide them a good service with right products, they can bring you more customers. Especially, if you are a sales person in a small town, you will struggle more if you are new to the town. In smaller towns, people buy from the sales people they have already dealt with it and it will be struggle for you to compete with sales people who have lived and worked there for years.

Building a personal relationship and staying in touch are the keys to keep your old customers. For example, I had worked with a sales person. He was a medium performing salesperson. I don't remember even once that he succeeded to hit her targets. His KDP rates were even lower than new salespeople. At gross margin rankings, he was always at the bottom among all salespeople because of his high discount percentage. He even used to go to manager to ask if she could a discount approval for a clearance for $80 clearance chair. Moreover, he did not know how to upsell and he did not have any passion but she did one thing exceptionally better than others:

Retaining old customers. He used to call his customers to ask how they like their products and if they have any questions or problems. He also used to build a personal relationship with them during the sale. Approximately, 20% of his sales were coming his old customers or their referrals. Selling his old customers were keeping his job secured. Otherwise, they had planned to fire him many times.

Some of important points to build a life time relationship with them when they are at your store:

* You must show them credibility and they must see that you know what you do and you are good at what you sell. They have to trust you so they can come back to you.

* Be completely honest about yourself and your products.

* You must build a personal relationship with them. Show them kindness, talk to them in a simple language without using jargons.

* Sell them according to their needs.

* Show them that you are similar to them. Pointing out your similarities with them will help you establish a long term relationship.

* You should attract them with your professional appearance. A proper and impressive appearance will gives them impression of professionalism and it will contribute to trustworthiness and respect on their mind.

After the sale:

* Be accessible to them. Make it as easy as possible for your customers to do business with you. Provide them your business card with your phone number. Tell them also that they can call you anytime regarding the problems or questions they may have after the sale.

* If they purchased from you, why don't you buy from them? If your customer has a clothing store, why not shop there sometimes.

* When you give them your business card after the sale, tell them that they can call you anytime for any problems they may have in the future regarding with the products they bought.

* Stay in touch. Call them once a while in the future and ask them if there is any problem with their products.

When you call them:

You must make sure your messages should be personal to

your customers and you should use their first name during call.

For example, Hello Michael, it has been long time I have not seen you. I hope you and your family are doing well. How's your new mattress? I am here to help you if you need any help. This is not a sales call so don't try to sell something them on phone. You should use these calls for the purpose of staying connected to them, not for making sales. Calling them will make them to think that you have not forgotten them and show them that you value them.

Summary:

Treat old customers like gold in vault. If they like you and your products, they will continue buying from you. Disconnecting with your old customers why one-time sales never turn into lifetime sales. If you do not connect, someone else will in your competition!

Follow- ups:

It is reality that you cannot close all of your customers whatever you do and how hard you tried. Some customers will delay their buying decision. Therefore, you should follow up with you customer who you could not close in their first visit. Ask their phone number and write on paper on what they were interested in purchasing. After a few days, contact to your customer to see when they are coming. If you have a promotion on your customer's products and tell your customers that I have great news for you, some of your products you were interested in are on sale now and they are going fast. When would you like to come? I been so busy and will be very busy in upcoming days but I will make a suitable time for you. If they say, they need still time to think. Don't give up. Call again and try again. If they still say they are not ready, you can try one more time. In my furniture sales, I always followed up with my customers and i used to close more than half of them with my calls back to them. When I used to sell appliances in a major appliance store, I had a couple, who were interested to buy $20,000 package. Wife was doctor and husband was a lawyer. I loved those customers. For those customers, they look for quality and price is not an issue for them. Their biggest objection is usually time since they are very busy. They were ready to purchase appliance package and money was not issue for them. They were building a new big house and they just wanted to finish their house built. This was their only objections. I wrote all of the products in the list with their prices, taxes, delivery price, taxes and total price. I understood that whatever I do, I would not be able to close that sale that day. I tried to get layaway deposit that I failed too. They were not completely ready to buy. I copied quote for myself and gave them original quote by attaching my business card . With a good smile, I saw them off even by opening outside door for them and said them bye. I waited a week to call them and I called. No answer. I waited another week and again no answer. I called them back in third week and they answered. I asked them how they were doing. He said I am sorry I saw that you called me several times. We had to go to Toronto and take care of our mother because she had a major traffic accident. I suddenly become like him and said i can understand you well. I had to take care of my mother for 2 weeks too because she was so sick and there was nobody to take care of her. After, I changed the subject smoothly into business. I asked him about his new house and asked how construction going on. I added: I saw your house last week while driving by there and it looks the best house in your neighbour. He said very thank you, we designed it from scratch and we are very happy with it. Again, I related his design to the appliance package they were interested and said: Well, before calling you, I talked to my store manager and region manager how we can help you about this appliance package and I believe that it is good idea to come to your home and see where you will put your appliances, I can also measure your spaces to make sure they will fit and with this chance, I can see your beautiful home. I mentioned you in the beginning of the book that sales are like a chess game and you plan your next move. I knew that they needed everything for their new house because they will rent their current house as furnished. I had already planned that I wanted to sell them mattresses, carpets, sectional, sofa with love seat, TV and coffee and end tables and several more things. I wrote everything down in my binder name by name, price by price, wrote three products in each category to show them. But I did not mention any of those to them. I needed to bring them into store for those but I need to focus on this appliance sale first. We got appointment for next day at 7 pm and I went to their home with in a nice dress. They greeted me at door; I shook their hands and went into home. I said that this house looks so beautiful from inside too. I said I like your smart design because you integrated your kitchen with your living room and you have big windows to have more sun coming in. In any opportunity I complimented their design to make them feel that I am like them. We went to kitchen area, we talked where we can put big Samsung Smart fridge, oven, dishwasher, microwave and we headed to laundry room to see where they plan to put washer and dryer. I measured all to make sure they will fit. Meantime, his wife made me a coffee and we talked about travel this time. I love travelling so it was a great way to get into more personal with them. They said they will go to Greece and Turkey in the summer. Since I know both countries well, I told them where to go, what to eat and where to shop. The things they should be careful etc... His wife even took notes what I told them. We decided to meet next day at 6:00pm at our store. Before leaving, I shortly mentioned indirectly by asking them: how will you furnish other rooms?

He said: We got a good deal for other stuff at another store. Next day, they came into our store at 6:00 pm. I made them sit in chair and asked them if they would like to drink something. They said coffee and I went to lunch room and made a coffee for them and brought back their coffees. They were ready to pay after chatting a few min more but I had to sell everything they need for their home. I could not let them going to competition and spent their money. I said I know you got a good deal at another store. I wonder what you are getting there. He put his hands in his pocket and took his quote from other store. They would buy one queen size mattress, one king size mattress, one leather and one fabric sectional, sofa set, 6 carpets, a 90-inch HD TV and one 55-inch HD TV, coffee and end table set, 8 chair dining table set. Their prices were fine but I was looking for their weaknesses in their quote. I noticed that they got two weaknesses in their quotes: Installation and quality. In their quote, they deliver everything to their house but they do not install right away. Moreover, they charge for installation. Also, they quote low quality mattresses in the list. I was not familiar with other furniture in the quote but their salesperson in the competition put product id numbers on quote. I asked him if you would like to have another coffee, they said sure. I said I will make you another coffee; by the way can I grab your quote? I will check something for you. He said sure. I quickly went to computer, put all of product id numbers in our competitions website, printed them out and made coffee for them quickly. I went back them with an happy face and gave coffees to them. I said I printed your products you had planned to buy from them. I am happy that they offered you great products but there are two major problems in their quotes. Wife asked what is that with a surprising gesture. I said installation and quality. I continued talking. I said: they do free delivery like us but they charge installation. They leave your furniture inside your house and leave. If you want installation, they charge you extra. Plus, they work with third party contractors but we have our own professional installation team who work only for us and they are fully insured during installation. If they accidentally damage your house during carrying heavy furniture, we are obligated to pay you for damage. They both said in same time we did not know that. The salesperson did not tell us that. I continued talking and said the mattress you are getting is not that good quality mattress. They are last year's models. We have a mattress on sale that supports your back all time, it conforms to your back, it eliminates motion transfer when both sleeping so when you turn around in mattress, other person is not disturbed. She said that's great, he moves a lot in the bed. I said lets go this mattress, and just lay down on mattress. They laid on mattress with the expensive pillows I gave them. I continued explaining benefits and features of the mattress. They loved it even my king size mattress was more $800 expensive than competition. He started to murmur his wife, let's buy everything from here. Wife said yes I agree. He said we loved this mattress and pillows. We are buying these two pillows, one queen, one king size mattress. Let's see other stuff to finish this. I had already known what to show them. I showed them all of products from their quote and sold all of them with warranties, plus I sold extra mattress sheets, 5 canvases, and an extra 6 piece queen bedroom package. Their total purchase was over $33,000! As you see how follow-ups can change your sales! Therefore, you must follow up your customers even if they did not buy. If you do not follow up, someone else in competition will follow up!

Don't badmouth your competition:

Badmouthing your competition shows that you are scared by your competition and shows you have weaknesses. I had a naive salesperson who was dealing with customer. Customer said: I went to another store and saw very similar Bosch dishwasher there but I wanted to check you out to see if you have the same of similar ones. The salesperson started to badmouth about the competition. Thank god, you came here. Their products suck; they have very poor quality customer service. They do not back up their products etc. Customer said him stop bashing your competitor. As sales professional, knowing our competitors should be an obligation but badmouthing them is not a good idea. Customers don't like negativity.

You should focus on advantages of your product and services and how those advantages and services make you different than your competition when customer says something positive about your competitor. Explaining differences do not mean to speak badly about your competition but it means to praise benefits of your products or services against your competitor. Unfortunately, many salespeople cannot stand the temptation to put down their competitors with their customers to sell. It is definitely a smart idea not to talk badly about your competition because it steals your sales pitch time on your competition rather than explaining your products and services. However, you should recognize the competition and without underestimating them, if you explain the advantages of your products or services show that you are educated, informed and classy salesperson. Obviously, your competition could and always can have better sides than your business but, it is your job to know differences and why you are better than them. In short, you should respect your competitors, and focus on your company strengths in your sales rather than bashing your completion.

Lying to customers:

Lying in sales is the worst offence you can commit .Trying to convince your customers with lies is the worst thing a salesperson can do. If you do not know something about a product, or about something, do not lie. Investigate it first and tell the customer truth. If you lie, you have to remember your lie, but if you tell the truth, you do not have to remember it. Lying in sales shows that you have not done your job properly to close your sale and show your weaknesses in the sales. Not only it can threat your job but also it can threat your company's reputation. Negative word of the mouth spreads immediately among people in your neighbour. Therefore, you should always tell the truth even if you lose a sale.

There are two types of lies: Black Lie and White Lie. The first one affects customers' lifetime involvement with you and with your store and the latter one does not affect much but still it is a dishonest way. If you tell your customers that our extended warranty covers power surge that is a black lie if your extended warranty does not cover it actually. If you tell your customers that I sold a lot of these fridges in last month to create social validation with your customer, it is a white lie. Let's be honest. More than half of salespeople make white lies. Lying in sales could be also in different forms. For example, a professional ethical salesperson will show his customers the best options to purchase according to their needs. A dishonest salesperson will show you only the products which pay him more commission. We should not forget that customers are intelligent like you. You can cheat once, two but not three times. We must make them feel that we are a good option for them to buy because we are here to take care of them and to offer them the best alternatives with trustworthiness.

A story from my insurance sales: I was one-day selling insurance door to door in rural in the south of New Brunswick in Canada. I saw a nice home on the uphill. I decided to try my chance and go there. I drove my car up on the hill. I parked my car and knocked on the door. While knocking on the door, I saw a pure naked woman taking shower in bathroom her back looking at me. She did not see that I saw her naked but her husband opened the door. He was on the phone busy with someone talking. I was not sure if he noticed that I saw her naked or not but he was on the phone talking. I felt so embarrassed but could not leave because he was looking at me and talking in the phone. I waited 5 minutes for him to finish phone call so i can talk to him and find an excuse to leave. I had already planned that when he hung up the phone, I would tell him that I lost my way and looking for this address by showing him an address. Before he hung up the phone, his wife finished taking shower and put her clothes on and came to the door. I had told her I am lost and looking for this address. She gave me the directions and I left from the home quickly. I kept cool and quiet during this event and pretended seeing nothing. Well, you will not see naked women in your store but you can always find excuses to leave from unwanted situations. If you see that they are talking each other about something private or they argue (that happens), just give them some space and leave.

Dealing with angry customers:

With these type customers, the key is not to argue with them. These are some tricks for you:

* You can apologize and accept responsibility even if it is not your fault.

* Stay calm and listen to them actively, reflectively and attentively.

* Don't get upset or emotional.

* Listen and empathize with them.

* Be clear them and let them know what you will do to solve their problems.

* Be sincere.

* Throw the ball to your managers if you can.

Choosing and judging customers:

We all know that looks matter for us. Once customer comes into store, you may like or not, they judge you by your look, by your dress and how you approach them. That's reality of the life that people judge each other for different reasons like the ones above. People have prejudice to some people. We cannot change that. You cannot judge your customers with their appearances, their weight, their height, their clothing style, their race, their language or with their negligence in their hygiene like smell. When a customer comes into your store, no matter what they look like, you must give the same service. We cannot guess right away in a second if they are going to buy or not for any new customers coming into store. A lot of sales people become picky according to customer types above. They choose or try to choose what customer they should help.

There is a good saying: "Don't judge the book by its cover". That is absolutely correct saying in sales. They can judge us but we cannot judge, we cannot have bias or prejudice or we cannot be picky which customer we should go for help. I will give you a good example how I closed a big sale in my junior years below:

A customer with muddy boots entered in the store. One of my co-workers saw that customer, he judged him with his appearances. He scratched his neck and asked me if I can help the customer.

I talked to customer; I built a wonderful rapport with him. He was a fisherman and just came back from the fishing. He was on the Atlantic Ocean for two weeks fishing lobsters and he was just paid. He gave me a list what he wanted:

- A 15 inches MacBook pro laptop for his daughter
- A 13 inches MacBook air laptop his son.
- Two iPads for younger kids.
- One 80 inches LED TV for his living room, one 65 inches LED TV for his bedroom.

- An high end Samsung Laundry Set, One dishwasher, a 29.5 Cu. Ft. Side-by-Side fridge and he wanted some other smaller items.

Making it short, total sale was over $11,000 and I sold extended warranty for all of major appliances and electronics.

Summary:

You must treat every customer the coming into your store with the same professional attitude without be choosy or picky. However, you should allow them to judge you with your professional appearance like a nice dress or suit on you without wrinkles.

Don't leave your customers alone:

I had a salesperson who was leaving customers in the middle of sale and going to talk on the phone. I had another salesperson who was leaving the customers to eat something in washroom by lying them that he is going to check something for them.

I will give you another real experience:

One of my salespeople were selling an expensive TV around $2,000. He did everything right and when customer seemed ready; he called another sales person and asked him if he can ring TV for him in cash register. He thanked to his customers, shook their hands, told them that he was going to have dinner and his friend will take care of the rest. How would you feel if someone did that to you?

Except emergency situations, you should never leave your customers in sales process. Once they are with you, they are yours until they leave. If you leave your customers to answer your phone or to do something private, you may end up forgetting what you have talked to them. A sale is like a complete basketball game. You must focus on your sale from the beginning to the end till they leave from your store. Even if you have other customers waiting for you, you cannot leave your customers to go to other customers. You can get permission from your customers to let other customers know that you will be with them after you are done with your current customers.

Don't hand flyers out your customers:

I worked at two furniture stores in same region. They were competition with each other. The first store banned salespeople to give flyers to customers at the entrance as long as they do not ask flyers. The other one was all right and allowing salespeople to give flyers right away at the entrance even if they did not ask one. Which ones are right? The first one or the latter? To answer this question properly, we should know why companies deliver flyers to homes and why you work as salesperson. They deliver flyers to homes to get attention from customers. They usually put cheap products or their best deals on their flyers to make customers bring your store to shop. Handing out your flyers to your customers depreciate of your status as salesperson. If they ask flyer right away, try to change subject or ask what you can do for them. Show them you know all of your products more than what on flyer and you know what best deals are. Even if you give flyer and if even they are interested at a cheap mattress, try to upsell a better mattress.

For the customers who come into your store with flyers on their hands, you should try to upsell what they came for initially. Also, you must try to cross-selling relevant products.

Use clipboards:

You should always use a clipboard when you are with your customers. When you use clipboard, you can write down all of the products, item numbers, taxes, total prices and their information. Show your customers on clipboard what they are buying today. Some customers may have buyer's remorse in cash register. Using clipboard and showing them total price is better idea than showing them everything on cash register. Using clipboard helps you when you make a one-time deal with your customers too. If you give them a deal, highlight with big numbers to show them how much they save after your deal and circle this amount for them to show them their savings. You can use a red ink pen to circle their savings too. Try to take their attentions on their savings in the purchase not on the total price.

Phone calls:

People sometimes go to your website or checking your flyers and they call you to ask you about certain products. It is harder to persuade people on phone than being in the store. You must try to bring them into your store. When you are on phone: try to keep short explaining the products and try to create scarcity. Tell them: it is better for me to explain and show the product if you can come into our store. Don't get into too many details on the phone. You can also tell customers that I am not sure that this product will be in the stock till you come (Sometimes, it happens, you sell out something until they come out), so I do not give guarantee that we will have one till you come. I can make an exception for you. If you come sooner today, I can reserve one for you to see it. Give your name to customer and take his/her name. Again, do not try to sell the product on the phone.

What not to share with your customers:

Some of the salespeople almost share everything to their customers including other customer's private life, your co-workers' private life, your company secrets and even your company' profit in the products. You cannot share everything with your customers. There are things that cross the line and those must not be shared. A good professional salesperson should have discretion and know what to talk and what to share.

I compiled some of the vital stuff that you should never share with your customers:

- <u>Don't gossip behind your co-workers with your customers:</u>Some customers love gossiping and talking. As a professional salesperson, you should and you must love talking but you should not love gossiping behind your co-workers with customers.

- <u>You should always back up your co-workers without annoying your customer:</u>Customer: I hate that salesperson over there. He did not treat me good last time. You: I am sorry for your experience with him. He is nice guy but sometimes it happens in our life. We are having bad experiences with salespeople. I will make sure that I will give you a great service to make your bad experience to forget. I had a salesperson named Melissa. She was a mediocre sales associate working in the same company for 4 years. She got no motivation, no positivism about the company, about the store manager, about other sales associates etc. She was the queen of the complainers. If a customer says something negative about a co-worker or about her company, she was jumping into conservation as whales jump in the oceans and telling her co-workers off to her customers. I had a customer who was bashing one of our sales associates. I was in distance changing price tags and heard what they had talked. Customer said that I dealt with Tina before and she was so annoying. She did not even listen to me. She talked so fast and she smelt smoking odour. Melissa said to the customer about X: she always does it. She had got complaints before. I would not deal with her again if I were you too. She exactly said that to her customer. Behaviours like this is totally unacceptable. When you work in a sales environment, you should be careful what to say about your co-workers. If you have some problems with your co-workers, there is no need to tell those problems to your customers. Whatever happens at your work, keep them privately. Think of them as one of your family members for 8 hours shift. Customers do not need to know anything negative about your co-workers. You must have the mindset that it is a privilege to represent your company to your customers. Gossiping behind your co-workers will rupture this mindset.

- <u>Try to evade religious or politic talks with customers</u>:I had a sales associate who was very religious and his wife homeschooling his children because his religion banned his kids going to school. He was trying to sell a dishwasher one of his customers who was priest in another church. Both broke into argument because of the religion. The sales associate forgot that he was a salesperson and started to argue with the customer. Of course, the customer did not buy but also complained about him to our head office. If your customers tell you that they will go to church or they go to church, you can ask them what church they go and you may know someone who goes to the same church with them and create this an opportunity to to build personalized rapport with them. Politics are the same. Some people love talking about the politics. When customers try to talk about politics, just listen to them and try to not put your opinions. I had a sales associate who swore at a famous politician while selling a chair to his customer. Customer was like him he used a vulgar word too. Another customer heard them and he started to argue with them. Keep your religious and politics opinion for yourself. You can use humour to make them relax when customer started to talk about politics. You can say something like: They only remember us when they need money. I pay my taxes and they stop bothering me or you may say: I love politicians. They are our best friends during the election and after the elections they disappear. Most of customers will agree what you have said.

- <u>Don't talk about your earnings:</u> Customers do not need to know how much you commission you make from their purchase. Just be like a politician and don't give a number. I make some money but not that much as you think. Try to change the subject. If you tell them how you make, they may be getting jealous, or they may make discount or they can ask you detailed questions about your commission rates.

- <u>Don't share negative things about your company, about your co-workers and about your customers on social networks:</u> I had a salesperson who wrote on her Facebook that she would sue to the company if they do not give her extra three days' vacation. Well, she was fired next day. Your friends on Facebook do not need to know anything negative about your company, your co-workers or about your customers. If you had a bad day, share it with someone you trust not with everybody on Facebook. There are many companies who watch what their employers say about them on social networks. Michelin is one of them. The famous French tire manufacturer Michelin fired one of his workers who criticized the working conditions of the company.

- <u>Don't talk about sex nor try to flirt with your customers:</u> I had a salesperson who used to talk about his sexual preferences with some of the customers. You might think it's okay to make an innocent comment to your customers about your sex life but your workplace is one place that you should never talk about sex with your customers. IN addition to sexual conservation, also don't try to flirt with your customers. For example, I had a salesperson who was a great salesperson. He was always on the top in sales rankings. He had an awesome narrative presentations and great salesman skills. When you listen to his sales presentations, you were as if you had been at the movie. He was hypnotizing.Unfortunately, he had a downside. When he dealt with men or couples, he was not taking much time to close the sale but when he was dealing single ladies, he was trying to flirt with them. It was taking more than double time for him to close sales to these female customers.Again one-day, he sold a TV to a single lady and told her that I will come to your home and set up TV for you which was against company policy. She said yes sure, we can have also a beer together. He went to her home, they had some fun together and later on, he set TV up for her and while he was setting up TV, he broke the screen. Since they were some drunk, she did not care about TV that night but next day she came back to store and demanded money back. She said your worker came at my home and while he was setting up TV, he broke it. Company paid the damages and they fired him right away. Customers make your company stay in the business.

Your work is not a proper place to flirt with your customers.

Summary:

These are some vital subjects that you should not talk with your customers. I did not describe all of them here like weigh, pregnancy, race, age etc. but you must keep your line with customers on your own.

Chapter 19: Financing

Financing your customers is very effective to close your sale for to overcome price objections. If your customer says that she cannot afford to buy then offering them financing is a great option.

<u>Right time frame for financing:</u>

Right frame is when you get first signal of price objections before doing the presentation but every customer and every sale is different and you need to adjust yourself accordingly. I had a lot of salespeople who could not adjust right time to do financing. I had a salesman who was terrible at this. He was selling everything at first by saying the customer: let's get what you want and we can do financing in the end. After he was selling bunch of products, he was doing financing application. He sometimes used to get disappointed because his customers were declined in credit check. Don't be like him. Do financing application before doing your presentation. I will give you one of my pitches for financing: Mr. Bruce, financing application will only take a few minutes. Mr. Bruce, if your father loans you free money and if he did not ask you back for 18 months with no interest, would you take it? I would sure accept that if he offered me that and pay him back in 18 months. I have even rich customers who use our financing option. They know that we don't charge any interest, there is no catch not bate in our financing. They use their money on something else instead of paying us today. This is the reason why they are rich. I also want to shortly explain you another financing option we have: It is 18 months with instalments each month. You pay it every month like car payments. Honestly, the first option is better for you because 9 out of 10 customers prefer the first option. In the first option, you can do monthly instalments but it is not mandatory etc.Doing financing on the computer with them also is a great step to build a personalized rapport with them. While you are doing financing with them on the computer, they may have tension and some anxiety because having financing means they are taking commitment to buy. Use humour and talk about the things they like or things they like do. Make them like you; make them as if you were their friends for years and sell today not tomorrow! Don't forget make them sit on a chair or on a bar stool so they can get relaxer.

Chapter 20: Avoiding Returns

Neither customers want to return something nor you want to see returns. It is time consuming for customers and for you. You also lose your hard-earned commissions because of returns. In addition that there is also opportunity cost for returns. For example, you may have helped customers one hour and when they return the products, not only you lose commission but also you lose your valuable one hour. You could be with someone else instead of being with those customers who returned the products and sold something they would not return. You cannot completely avoid returns but you can reduce them.

You can avoid returns in two ways:

1: Sell the right things

2: After the sale

3: Sell the right things:

Some of salespeople have a tendency to sell products that their customers don't even need. These types of salespeople have too much greed to sell or they don't know how to qualify customers.

In addition, some customers may be embarrassed to say

no to salespeople. They may have embarrassment to say you no, and they may buy and return their purchase later on. For instance, I had a salesperson who sold the customer the things she did not even need. Customer came back to the store and returned the whole purchase. She told that I could not say no to him because he was so pushy and I did not want to be embarrassed. He tried to sell me more than what I need. She returned approximately $5,000 worth purchase because of him. I had another salesperson who oversold the customer and customer returned some of the products. They said that she was so nice to us. We could not say no to her so we bought everything. We did not need sofa and area rug so we are returning them now. As salesperson, you should be aggressive and pushy without customer noticing it. If you cross the line, if you sell what customers don't need or will not need, it will cause buyer's remorse and a return. It will also hurt you when you see a big return in your sales report. You should give opportunities to your customer to experience your products. You must qualify customers for right products and you should let them touch, feel, try, play with the products you sell. By doing those help your customers to be informed about the products they are buying and minimizing their returns.

2. After the sale: It's a very good idea to make a follow-up call to your customer to see how their product are working and if they have any problem. Calling them also helps you establish a continuous relationship with your customer. In some instances, whatever you do, you cannot prevent returns. They are going to return regardless. But you may prevent some of returns by learning why they return.

I will give you a good example how a cleaner prevented a return: I was flying from Munich to Frankfurt in Germany. I went to airport and as usual we always tend to get hungry at airports and in planes. My flight was with low cost airline Ryan Air .I dropped at McDonalds and wanted to get something before taking off. There were people waiting in line, I waited my turn and started to wait for my food. Meantime, a gentleman approached cashier and told her that he wanted to cancel his order because it was taking a lot of time. Cashier started to process his refund in cash register. A cleaner who was cleaning floors heard their conservation.

He asked him:

- What airlines are you flying with?

- He said I will fly with Ryan Air

- He said they don't give food in the plane and you will be very hungry in the flight because of lower air pressure and your flight will be a long flight to Egypt. You should not cancel your order. You will be very hungry in the plane. - Customer said yes I agree and he did not cancel the food and waited 5 minutes more to take his order.

I don't know what your store policy could be when your customer comes into the store to return. The right way is that customer service rep calls you to deal with your customer again. Once you have opportunity to deal with your customer again, you will have another opportunity to talk to them and to learn the reason behind their return. When I was sales manager, I prevented many returns by just talking to customers again. You can do that too. Maybe your customer had thought that the product was too expensive for her. Her husband or some friends, relatives said to return it. You can either try to explain benefits if the product or you can try to downgrade her purchase by showing them other options. When you try to prevent their returns, be always positive with smiling face and do empathy with them. It relaxes them and makes them to think again.

Don't say:

-I don't think that product is expensive. We sell it at cost etc. They don't want to hear that.

Say:

-I am sorry that you feel that expensive. We work hard to make money and I can understand your feeling but I have great news. We have another product that just came in our store. I did not have a chance to show you that day. You would definitely love that product. We can quickly check it out and after that we can continue finish your return process that takes only few minutes. Show that product to your customer and try to persuade her to exchange. It sometimes works. You got nothing to lose but save your sale and your commission!

Chapter 21: How to Upsell and Cross-sell

Both of these sales techniques are great ways to maximize your sales and your pocket. Let's go over them to see why they are important for us:

Upselling:

Upselling is basically a practice of encouraging customers to purchase a comparable higher-end product than the one they are interested in.

Upselling examples:

- A restaurant cashier asks you if you want to buy a Triple Cheeseburger with $1.00 more.

- If a customer wants to buy 40-inch TV, you are trying to sell 50-inch TV.

- Customer comes to buy an cheap recliner chair whose purchase price is $299.99 and you try to an higher-end recliner chair whose purchase price is $399.99

- You book an hotel and the receptionist asks for a breakfast for only $19.99 that normally would cost $39.99 if you bought it online.

How can you upsell to your customers?

I will give you some tricks how you can upsell any customer. You will have always customers who come in your store to buy cheapest products. I am looking for cheapest mattress, I am looking for cheapest fridge, I am looking for the cheapest sofa etc. We don't like to hear when they say the cheapest. It makes some salespeople help them reluctantly. There are some tricks to overcome these types of customers. For example, when you have customers coming into your store and pointing out you a cheap mattress on front page in your flyer, you can tell your customer excitingly: this mattress is very good mattress at this price. We sell it a lot after it has gone on sale. I will happily help you. You take the customer to the mattress she is interested. Explain features and benefits and tell your customer: I don't want you to make a wrong decision even if this mattress is really good deal at the moment. When you go to shoe store, do you buy the first shoes that you saw in shelves or do you check and try other shoes too? Or would you decide to get marry to someone in your first date? Probably not, I have another mattress which is way better than this mattress and which is also 60% off.

Take her to the mattress and let her lie down and explain her by comparing this new mattress with the old one. Focus on why this mattress is better than the other one: I mentioned you that the first mattress I showed you has only 300 pocket coils but this mattress has 860 pocket coils. When you have more coils, you will have a better support for your back which will also give you a better sleeping quality etc. You only pay $149, 99 more and you get way better mattress. Don't you think that your sleeping does not worth $149, 99 more? Without stopping, continue talking and say: I would definitely go for this mattress by paying only a little less and wait for customer's reaction. In another example, I had a customer who came to buy a cheapest fridge with flyer on his hands. He was an old a farmer. I told right away him with a smile that you know about the fridges. That is really good fridge. I explained features&benefits to him and I asked him that what brand tractor do you have? He said of course John Deere. I said I will show you John Deere of the fridges. The first one was Massey Ferguson. I took him the second fridge which was $500 more than the first one. I compared the new fridge with the old one with examples and he bought the second fridge. When you have these types of customers, always pick two more products in your mind with higher price and try to upsell higher-end products. Focus on quality, features&benefits when you try to upsell and do comparisons as I did in the mattress example. The comparisons could come from real examples as I did in the fridge sale. In addition that upselling is also a great sales tactic to increase your customers' happiness by adding more value with quality and it can also help you build deeper relationships with your customers.

An upselling story from me:

One-day I was buying oranges at a street vendor in Istanbul. He was selling them for 4 liras for per kilogram. I asked him one two kilograms oranges that were costing 8 Turkish liras. (4 liras for per kg). He started to put oranges in the bag. He said we should make this even. I will give you half more kg and make it even to 10 liras. I said sure. I gave him 10 liras and left. The next day, I went to him to buy 1 kg apples. Apples were 3.5 liras. I told him to give me 1kg apples please. He again used the same trick. While putting apples into bag, he asked me that let's make this even to 5 liras. I will put extra half kg for you. I said sure. He put half more kg into bag. After I finished, I watched another sale. He asked customer that let's make this even. I will give you 5 kgs instead of 4 kgs and we will make it even. Customer said yes to him and he paid him 20 liras instead of 16 liras. I used his trick a lot in my sales to make customers spent more on especially on mattress or furniture sales. For example, I had a young customer. She bought a sofa from me with warranty. Total cost was approximately $1440. I showed her two pillows that match with sofa. I told her that I forgot showing you pillows. These are the pillows match with your sofa and let's make this even. With these two pillows, total price will be even $1500. She said yes sure let's do it. This technique works if you sell relevant products to customers. Try it, you will see it works.

Cross-Selling: While upselling is an attempt to sell higher-end products at higher price, cross- selling involves selling related or products that are complement to each other.

Some of cross-selling examples:

- A restaurant cashier asks: Would you like fries with your burger that only costs $ cents extra.

- If a customer wants to buy 40-inch TV, you are trying to sell power surge protector with it.

- You buy a pack of cigarette and cashier asks you if you want to buy a lighter for only $2.

How to make a cross-selling?

In cross-selling we try to sell relevant products. Think of these examples and what we can sell relevant products with them:

- Mattress: mattress protector, pillow, bed frame, mattress sheet etc.

- TVs: Power surge protectors, a TV stand, sound system etc.

Before trying to do cross-selling, you must know relevant products to pitch and you must only pitch relevant products after you succeeded to sell the main item. For example, you are selling a TV and if your customer did not say yes to buy yet, don't try to sell power surge protector without managing to sell TV first. Of course, you can plant the seeds to sell power surge protector during the presentation. I had a salesperson who was selling the metal bed frame first for the mattresses he was trying to sell. It is a wasting effort. Sell the main product first not complement product. I will give you a good example for cross-selling one of my sales: I had a customer who came to buy a 13-inch MacBook Pro for his son. His son was starting at university the next month and he wanted to get a MacBook Pro for him. Selling the laptop was like easy cake. He had already decided to buy it. I pitched the warranty and he bought warranty for it. I pitched computer setup which was costing $99 and he bought it. I needed to sell laptop bag and an high-end wireless gaming controller which I had already planned but did not pitch him. I told them that let's go to cash register to ring the sale. While we were going to cash register, I pretended to drop the laptop from my hands. The father said that be careful, don't break it. I said I broke a laptop last month by accident on display (I did actually), by the way I forgot showing you something very important. He said what are you going to try to sell me now? I said I was not going to sell you anything but I will show you something that will protect his laptop. We stopped at laptop cases section. I said him that you pay tons of money to buy this laptop but we forgot the most important thing: a laptop case and I asked him if he uses snow tires. He said yes. I said you use snow tires because you don't want to have accident in the winter because they keep you on the road. Laptop bag is like snow tires. It will protect his laptop when he walks from class to class at university. He said write it down too. I said he mentioned that he plays video games and we also forgot adding a gaming controller. He did not have any objections and asked how much? I said it is only $159, 99 and we sell it a lot to MacBook Pro customers because it is high-end product like your MacBook. He said write it down too. We went to cash register to ring the sale and he asked me that do you want to work for me? I said I do make good money here. He said you can make $200,000 at working us. I said what is your job? He said I am general manager of GM dealership here and he gave me his business card. He said that you are great person and you did everything to make a cross-sell. I kindly said that I will think of your offer and let you know. As you see that cross-selling is not just to sell anything to increase your sales. I want you to understand how cross-selling can be implemented by giving you one more example. I want to make sure that it will stick in your mind so you will never forget cross-selling when you sell to your customers, so I want to share one more stories with you:

A cross-selling story: A passionate a naive village boy with no sales experience applies for a sales job at a biggest boat dealership in an averaged sized city.

The sales manager calls him for interview and he asks him: Have you ever sold?

The boy: Yes, I sold beef cattle to butchers.

Manager says: Good, you start tomorrow. The boy starts the next day and he sells to one customer. The sales manager calls him in the evening and asks: How many sales did you do today?

- Boy says: I did one sale.

- The manager says: What one? Did you do only one sale? Others made average 5 sales today. How much was your total sale?

- The boy says:$110,000

• The manager was shocked and asks him: how did you do that?

- The boy says: I had a customer who came to buy a small size fishing rod. I showed him a bigger size and he bought it. Then, I asked him that where he would fish. He said he would fish on the south shore. I told him that it is not good idea to fish on the south shores because there are cliffs that are interspersed with trees over there and filled with large mossy rocks. Then, I showed him a luxury boat. I explained him why he should buy this yacht and he bought it. Afterwards, I saw that he needed a SUV to pull his boat and he bought it.

Summary:

I don't want you to get me wrong that sole objective of upselling and cross-selling is only to increase your sales by selling anything to your customers. In upselling, you should sell something more quality by adding value. In cross-selling, you should only sell what they need or may be relevant to their purchase. You don't want your customers to have buyer's remorse by buying all bunch of stuff which they would not need. In addition that both upselling and cross- selling are great sales principles to increase your customers' loyalty. In addition that both will help you deepen your relationship with your customers to build a lifetime relationship with them. Both of these sales principles also have obvious benefits for any company and for any salesperson: more revenue for your company and better paycheque for you. Your customers will feel more satisfied with you and with your company that can able to cover all their needs. Lastly, both of these principles are to perfect principles to improve your persuasion skills.

Chapter 22: Extended Warranty Sales

Selling extended warranty requires extra skills than selling main item products. You are going to have more objections in extended warranty sales than selling the main item. Warranty sales will require more persuasion skills than selling the products because your customers already came into your store to buy a specific product or products but most of them did not even think of buying warranty before coming. They are just conditioned themselves to buy the main item such as fridge, TV, mattress etc. saw so many terrible salespeople including top writers who thought they were the best because they sold more than anyone but they could not even sell extended warranties. Any salesperson including top writers, if they cannot sell extended warranty, I don't count them as a good salesperson.

<u>I had a top writer co-worker who was asking her customers:</u>Would you like to have extended warranty? Do you want a warranty? These questions were asked by a top writer not by a low performing salesperson!To be able to sell extended warranty, you must listen to them actively to pinpoint their weaknesses and plant the seeds during your presentation. For example, I had a

couple customer with three small children. They needed a laundry set. Before coming, they checked all of the laundry sets and decided to buy a Samsung laundry set. They had their model number and they had a lot of information about the laundry set. While I was checking the laundry set in our website, I heard they were talking quietly about one of their youngest child allergy problems. Samsung laundry set was $1799, 99 and it did not have steam. They had a weakness. Their child had allergy problems. This was an opportunity to sell another laundry set that has a steam washing technology. I told them that this is great laundry set and explained features and benefits. I added that although it is great machine, it lacks of one important technology: steam. We have an LG laundry set which comes with steam on both machines. I explained why steam is better, what it does, how it kills bacterias, how it removes odour from clothes etc. Well, they liked what I explained them about LG laundry set but they had still small hesitations. I also took one more step by showing a small demo video about its sanitization technology. They decided to buy my LG laundry set which was $400 more than Samsung. While explaining features and benefits I planted seeds to sell warranty by saying: it comes with 1 year limited warranty, and I would definitely buy warranty since you have small kids and continued explaining about the product.After they decided to buy, I pitched the warrant by focusing on their children. I said you live in rural area far from everything. I cannot imagine not doing laundry when especially you have three children. This laundry set is great but as you know when cars get older, they break more and people too. Look at me, I am older with grey hair and turned toward the man and said: we are at almost the same age but you got a perfect pure black hair and you look younger than me. They smiled and I smiled. Even new cars break down so I want to make sure that you will have laundry set running in your home for your children all the time. With our warranty, you don't have to deal with manufacturer but you deal with us directly. You don't have to call those foreign based call centres to and try to understand their accent whose accent worse than me (smile). If we cannot repair it or if it is too expensive for us to repair, we don't even bother repairing it. We will you brand-new one etc. You may an handy guy or you may have someone who knows how to repair it but parts are very expensive. If you need to change the drum, it would cost you a fortune. We will deal with your laundry from the beginning to the end. I cannot even imagine that what you would do without washing your kid's clothes. To keep it short, they bought the extended warranty by agreeing my points about their children.

Summary: I could write 200 pages how to sell extended warranties because I was always number 1 salesperson in warranty sales in any place I worked. Three things are the most important to sell extended warranty:

- 1: Building a personalized rapport

- 2: Listening, using humour and giving them real solid examples.

- 3: Focusing on their weaknesses and your products' weaknesses.

Selling warranty will also increase your persuasion skills. If you cannot sell the warranty that means: you are buying hamburgers without French Fries and a drink. Make it a complete sale, sell extended warranty. In another book, I will focus on warranty sales more with solid examples. I don't count any salesperson as successful salesperson if they cannot sell extended warranty including the top writers. A sale without selling extended warranty is not a complete is a vague sale.

Chapter 23: The Principles of Persuasion

Sales jobs require persistence and having persuasion skills. Of all the sales skills needed to be a successful salesperson, persuasion is probably one of the most important. If you want to change your customers' mind and if you want to get them buying your products, persuasion is essential principle to succeed. Having effective persuasion skills will help you influence your own point of view on your customers and make them adapt your point of view. According to famous psychologist Robert Cialdini, there are 6 important principles to persuade your customers.

1. Social validation

2. Authority

3. Reciprocity

4. Commitment(Consistency)

5. Likability

6. Scarcity

1. Social validation:

Our brain tries to make decisions based on the right thing. It observes what most people do. For example, if you see 10 people running on the street toward opposite direction, your brain will not weight different options but it will try to urge you to run toward the same direction together with those 10 people. You have probably shopped at Amazon. If you want to buy something, before buying it, you check how many good reviews it has. If reviews are good, and if other buyers socially validate the product, it makes you decision faster to buy. In another example, when you are in a concert, you clap your hands when all other people do because other people urge your brain to clap your hands. We like to do what others do: Just supposed there are two vendors selling burgers next to each other at the same price and lets name them A and B. You are already hungry and you need a quick fast food. While walking on the street, you see two burger vendors in distance. You are not sure which one makes better burgers because both are very busy with customers packed on the front of them. Suddenly, you see your neighbour Jack, and his wife

Michelle and at vendor A. You think that if Jack&Michelle eat here, then A should be better than B and you decide to eat at A. While waiting for your turn to come, you say hello to them and chatting with them. Let's change this example to opposite direction: B is busy. There are a lot of customers waiting to get a burger at B. A is not busy at all. Nobody is waiting. Where would you eat? A or B? You would probably buy at B because many people chose B over A. Sales are the same. Customers like to hear social validation. They want to decide according to the public consensus. For example, I sold a $16,000 a complete home package to a couple from a small town in Saskatchewan in Canada. Husband was a principle at high school and his wife was an history teacher. They were well known and well respected professionals. I asked them if I could use their name to give reference to my customers from your town. They approved that. When I had customers from their town, I always used this couple's names to build a personalized rapport and to sell. Since it was a small town, everybody knew them. I closed a lot of sales thanks to this couple. In another example, when I used to sell door-to-door insurance for an insurance company, I used to give references to my prospects on the door. For example, hello, sorry for disturbing you at this beautiful day, I am Eco coming from Combined Insurance. I was just at Michelle's and at Eric's house and I just wanted to see you for few minutes. I am just here to tell you a few important things. Don't worry I will not try to sell you anything (Actually I would).Giving them references in the town made them easier to trust me and reduced their tension to allow a stranger like me to get into their house. You should always ask your customers if you can use their name to give references to your customers from their neighbourhood. To have social validation with your customers, you can also relate your experiences or examples to the subject, your previous customers' experiences and public opinion. I will give you another example from my sales how I did social validation with one of my customers to sell him a washer: He needed 5.0 cu. ft. front loader washer. We had only two in our display. One was LG and other was GE. They were very similar to each other but GE was $100 cheaper than LG. Moreover, GE had sanitizing option that LG did not have it.I checked our stock levels and saw that LG was in back order and we would have it back approximately 2 months later. Customer needed it in a week. Therefore, selling LG was not option for me. Customer did not like GE brand because he had GE before. He said he had very bad experience with GE and his GE washer was very loudly. I told him that GE is great choice for you. It is $100 cheaper; it has sanitizing option which LG does not have it. It is a great option to kill bacterias with its steam technology. He resisted and said no. Of course, I would not let him go to another store and buy washer from there. I managed to build personalized rapport with him and used humour to do that. I also kept my balance and did not make him feel that I am a pushy salesperson. Whatever I did, whatever explained to her, he said no.I told him that I know you will not buy but I will show you something very important for your future knowledge when you buy a washer. I know you do not like GE brand but brands has nothing to do with bad experiences. He had a Toyota car. I asked him how he likes her Toyota.He said: I love it and I always buy Toyota. I asked him that do you know that Toyota has recently recalled approximately 1.4 million Lexus and Prius vehicles over faulty airbags. He said yes I know that. I said there are over 30 different Toyota models from Toyota Yaris to Lexus. Although Toyota recalled 1.4 million vehicles, Toyota is still number 1 auto seller in the USA because they make great cars and people like its quality.She said you are right and she became softer in her objection about GE. I said GE is the same. It has over 20 different types of washers and they make great washing machines. You bought only 1 out of 20 models and you did not have a good luck with it but that does not mean that all of GE washers are bad. She nodded his head. I could see from his eyes that her objections were reduced more but he still seemed not ready to buy. So I told him that I will show you something more quickly and after that you can decide to buy or not. I went on Amazon website and searched GE washer on search bar with model number and I reopened another page and searched LG washer.(I already knew GE got better reviews than LG and both were at the same price with ours).GE washer got 4.5 stars and LG washer had only 3.5 stars on Amazon. I showed him reviews of other people, and I found a review that says this is one of the quietest machines I have had. I did read that that part loudly for her and she started to change her mind. I took one more step and went on consumerreports.org and compared noise level of two washers and GE washer got better ranking for noise levels too. She said that's enough validation. You can take my money. She bought it with 4 years warranty and with installation. As you see my persistence paid out. She did not want to trust to my opinion but when she saw other people's opinions, she changed her mind.

Summary:

Customers have grown to distrust brands and salespeople. They like to see the public opinion, or want to hear similar names they know and who bought from you. If you can have social validation with your customers, they will trust you more and they will buy from you. Close the sale today, not tomorrow!

2: Authority:

Customers usually look for experts or symbols of authority to guide them and shape their decisions. With recognizing authority, they tend more likely to change their behaviours because they know that they are dealing with a salesperson who has authority over them and knows his subject better than them. For example, if I have an overweight problem and if my doctor tells me, I will have to have surgery, if I do not lose weight, then I will follow his advice and I will try to lose weight. Because he knows his subject better than me and I believe that he has authority over me. You can create authority on your customers on variety ways and proving them that you are an experienced sales person and you know your products well. For example, if you have a customer who believes that your product does not have good quality, you can tell your customer: I have over 10 years' experience working here and have sold this product a lot of times. With my best knowledge, it is one of the best in the market. When you say 10 years, your customer automatically thinks that you know what you sell and try to accept your authority on that specific product. After that you can tell why it is the best with your knowledge. Sometimes, you will have customers with you had difficulties to close your sale. You tried hard but you could not. Instead of letting them leave, you can call one of your co-workers or your sales manager to close the sale or extended warranty sale. Introduce your co-worker or sales manager to your customers by saying: Arthur has worked here for 8 years and he is more experienced in warranty sales so he will explain in details how our extended warranty works. Your customer suddenly thinks that this man is more experienced and knows more than you, so it is better to listen to Arthur to see what he will tell about your warranty. When your customers feel insecure, or when they do not trust you, they usually look for testimonials from a "person with authority on the subject" as a guide. For example, there is a company called Bedgear. This company sells performance bedding accessories such as high-end moisture wicking mattress sheets, pillows and mattress protectors. Their pillows used to range from $79.99 to $199.99 and mattress protectors were ranging between $59.99 and $249.99. Selling them was not easy sell. When my customers did not want to buy because they were overpriced, I had one more card in my sales arsenal. I was saying: I know you are not interested in buying but I will steal 4 more minutes in your life. I used to open 4 minutes long a quick BedGear demo video that was aired on TV. I can tell you that I sold a lot of mattress protectors and pillows thanks to this short video. Because my customers trusted BedGear sales associate's knowledge in the video and they used to buy after watching this short video.

Summary:

In sales, we must use authority all the time to build confidence with our customers. If you can make your customers perceive authority over them, they will more compliant with your request.

3. Reciprocity

The basis of this principle is very simple: If you do

something for someone, they will feel obligated to return the favour back to you and do something for you. It is an almost automatic reaction. People feel obligated to repay favours. For example, if your car is broken down and if your friend drives you to work, you would feel obligated to repay this favour back to him in the future. We are conditioned to do a favour to people who did a favour to us.

We use reciprocity on daily basis on many occasions:

* Your friend invited you to his wedding and you feel obligated to invite him to your wedding.

* You go to a restaurant and waitress gives you a small gift like a pen and it makes you feel obligated to give tips or even more tips than normally you would give.

* If you pay your friends' bill at the restaurant, you will not forget this and you will be willingly to pay next time when you go to restaurant together.

* Retailers or food companies know giving away a little free product for customers to test in the stores.

When someone does us a favour, we feel that a debt is created with that person, and we should repay the debt at some point. The principle of reciprocity can also occur in sharing your feelings and emotions.

For example, if you share your intimacies with your best friend who has given you confidence, he will tend to feel obligated to tell his intimacies. You can apply the principle of reciprocity in many forms at your work. For example, I used to use the principle of reciprocity many times at my sales. I had always a stock of water, Coke and Pepsi as cold and as warm in our warehouse to give my customers. I will give you two specific stories how you can use this principle at your sales:

The first story:

I had an old couple over 75s, who I just saw in our driveway. They were walking slowly into our store. I walked to our entrance and I opened the door for them and I held the door till they got in. They said very thank you, we are old as you see, and we cannot walk fast as you do because you are young. I told them with a smile. No, you are not old; you look very young and happy. I am getting more and grey hair every day. They smiled.

She said that I am not happy because he made a mess last night. He broke window glass by accident and she smiled. They told me that they came to check TVs and they will go to Wal-Mart to check their TVs after here. I said well, you are at right place at right time with right sales person. We have a sale going on and I have some great TVs for you. We made it to TV section but he was so tired and I saw that he was sweating. There was an end table in our TV section and I told them, just a second please, I will come back. I suddenly grabbed two chairs from furniture section and brought them to sit. I grabbed two chairs and pulled up them and I said please sit down to have a rest for a while. They said thank you and they were very happy about this. They sat down. I told them I will bring my binder to see what TVs are on sale and left. I went to fridge and took two bottled water. I said them I can see that you are sweating so I brought water for you surprisingly. They liked that. I said it is cold water but if you wish I can bring warmer one. Both said it was fine. We preferred cold water. It has been hot. They drank their water while sitting. I start talk to them about their lives. I asked questions, I showed my curiosity. I asked how many kids, how many grandchildren they had, what their job were etc. They liked my conservation. Subject opened subject. Finally, I had very good personalized rapport with them. They were in buying mood. It was time to show TVs. Old man said that you show her TVs. I am very tired. You are a good salesman; I trust your choice and told her to follow me. You go Jamie with him. She followed me. I started to show her TVs and narrowed her choice by asking her qualifying questions. Since she did not know much about TVs, I did not get into too many technical talks. After narrowing to her choices, I let her watch a short movie on an LG TV. She liked LG TV. She said I like it and she called her husband. Jason, I liked this one. Jason said let buy it here honey. This guy is nice guy. Nobody will help us like him at Wal-Mart. They would not even offer us a nail at Wal-Mart but he allowed us to sit and he brought us water without even asking. She said we are buying it. I told her that you are making a good choice by buying. I would buy this TV too. Since I did not sell extended warranty yet, I continued using humour with them. Do you know what was the best choice have you made in your life? She said I don't know, you tell me. I said you have a wonderful husband and he was the best choice you had made in your life. She laughed and he laughed. Do you want to know what the second best choice in your life is? She said no. I said buying this TV is the best second choice you are making now. She again laughed. After confirming TV sale, I sold extended warranty, TV stand and power surge protector with no objections at all. I also used a lot of humour during my sale.

The other story: I love chocolates and most of people love them too. When I used to sell insurance door-to-door, I had always three types of German chocolate bars in my binder that I used to buy from eBay Germany since they did not sell these chocolates in the North America. One of them was very low calories with pistachios; the other two were with hazelnuts and almonds. I was putting them on the front face of my binder so my customers can see them when I opened my binder. They usually asked what they were and from where you bought them. If they did not ask, I was offering them to eat my chocolates after a few minutes passed. Usually, they were accepting my offer to eat my chocolates. While they were eating my chocolates, I was building a personal rapport with them by talking the things they liked to talk about. Once I made their mood well enough, I was doing my pitch to sell my insurance products. I don't remember any customer who did not buy insurance from me after eating my chocolates. It did work. I made tons of money thanks to these chocolates.

These pro-social behaviours can help you nurture more positive relationships with your customers:

- Opening the door for your customers at the front entrance.

- Taking one more extra step by opening a product box for them to show the product if it is not on display.

- If they want to use washroom, taking them to washroom by turning on the lights and opening the washroom door for them.

- Grabbing or pulling up chairs for customer to sit down.

- Offering them a napkin if they sweat.

- Offering them something to drink. As I used to.

Summary:

If you make your customers feel special and unique by offering them something, then you finished almost half the sale. When you customers respond your favour, continue building a personalized rapport with them until they are in perfect mood to listen your sales pitch. Use this principle, it does work and I made too many sales by using this simple principle.

4. Consistency (Commitment)

The principle of commitment and consistency is deeply built-in our brain. This principle states that human public behaviour remains consistent over the long term. We want to keep our promises and commitments, particularly if we make them publicly. People tend to be consistent in all areas of life such as on their attitudes, on their habits, on their values, on their opinions and on their promises. Consistency is a very important adaptive behaviour. Learning customers' previous purchasing habits gives us an helpful shortcut advantage. Once a person made a decision in the past, the person takes a stand, and the person tries to make all future behaviour by matching his/her past behaviour. So it is very important for us to know their past purchases. For example, I am a fan of Adidas Pure Boost running shoes. I have had 6 pair of them so far. The last one I bought torn off after two months but still I went to buy the same shoes because I made six times commitments and has begun to behave in a way that is consistent my previous commitments because I think these are the best shoes for me to run. According to Robert Cialdini, this principle implies that people tend to be consistent or be coherent with something they said previously. He says: "once people have made a choice or taken a stand, they will encounter personal and interpersonal pressures to behave consistently with that commitment. Those pressures will cause us to respond in ways that justify our earlier decision. "In most cultures around the world, consistency is seen as a valued personal trait by people. People are not consistent, seen as unreliable, deceptive and untrustworthy. Consistency supports our decisions. For example, when we end our relationship, our brain tries to support this idea. Our brain tries to make us believe that we have done right thing to break up and it was the best option for us to break up. According to Dr. Robert Cialdini, when you encourage people to make a little, a voluntary, and an active commitment in public, they would more likely to keep greater commitments. Therefore, when you try to influence your customers, you should try to find ways and methods to influence your customers by making them voluntary, active and public commitments. I will give you to four good examples about this principle:

1st example:

I used to use our layaway policy to close sales by taking small layaway deposits. I used to take small amounts of deposits from my customers to make them commit to buy. I remember I even got $10 commitment from one of my customers who came back next week and paid the remaining $8960. (That company used to allow accepting layaway deposits up to $10).

2nd example: I had a customer who waited about 30 minutes because we were so busy. He wanted to buy a TV but he did not have much time left because he had meeting soon. I approached him and calmed him down. I took him TV section and I showed him TVs. He said I read reviews about this TV. It was a Samsung TV. This TV got very good reviews. I showed him the TV he was interested in. After explaining him features and benefits, he said he does not have time, he has to go. I will come back another time. I told him that this TV sells fast since it is on sale. You pay me 25% of total price; I will hold it for you. He resisted my offer. He was about to leave. I said him just a second please. I brought my sales manager to make him to think that he has more authority than me. My sales manager knew the situation and told him that I will make exception for you and you pay us only 10% of total price and we will hold it for you. He said there are only two left. Customer accepted the offer and he left. He came next day, paid the remaining amount; he bought warranty with it too. He could be one of "those be backers" otherwise.

3rd example: I wanted to sell an high-end mattress to a customer and she thought it was expensive. She did not have financing either. She said she does not have enough money on her to pay for it. She said I will be paid next week to buy it. I said her that I would like to make a favour for you since you are very valuable customer. You pay me 25% of the total price, I will keep it for you and I will also lock the sale price when you are back. Since they are on sale, the price will change soon. You can come back anytime and pay the remaining balance. I called her twice in two weeks to remind her she has payment with us (it was company policy to call customers who had layaway deposit at us) She did not answer my calls. I called her one more time at third week and she said she was away so she could not answer. She said she will come tonight. She came back and bought mattress with mattress protector and with two pillows.

4th example: I had a customer who said that if you can hold the product for him for next four hours, he will come back and buy it. I told him that we don't hold the products if you don't pay us deposit. He did not want to pay deposit. I wanted him to publicly commit so I took him to my store manager. There were two more sales people and luckily one of salespeople knew him. He told my manager that he will come back if you hold the product for him. My manager said, we will do exception for you. Normally, we don't do that since people don't come back when we used to that. He said I will come back. He left and he came back four hours later and bought $4000 worth appliance package.

Summary: As you see, making your customer involved in a small commitment can help you increase your sales. In addition that you can make them publicly express their commitment as I did in last example. Making small commitments from your customers trigger the principle of consistency, making your customers easier to say yes to subsequent requests. Even giving your customers a detailed quote with your handwriting is a commitment. You can keep one copy of it and you can call your customers to see when they are coming back. They know that you wrote a quote for them and they feel more committed. You cannot leave things up to chances, probabilities or assumptions. Using this important principle in your sales will lead you close more sales. If you could not make them commit then you cannot expect your customers to commit ton you.

5. Likability (familiarity) I explained this important principle at the beginning of the book to sell yourself to customers before selling your products. Since this is the most important principle for me, I will shortly explain it in a different way. When you talk to customers, be like their friends. If they have any problem, listen to their problems. If they have something nice on them like a nice dress, give a nice compliment about her or his dress. With compliments, you can transfer your positivism on them. I liked your shoes. Where did you buy them? They look gorgeous on you. Who would not like to hear this? If you give compliments, you also create an opportunity to build a personalized relationship faster because they will more willing to open up their lives. Wear nice, look nice. You cannot cheat your customers with a bad appearance. Always look professional on your customers to increase your credibility. Don't buy cheap clothes. Clothes are your investment so buy nice dresses or clothes for you to wear at work. Be curious about their lives, ask questions about their lives and share your experiences for the things you are in common with them. Again, if you can sell yourself first, you can sell anything.

6. Scarcity:

If something is not scarce, it is not desired. Creating scarcity is a powerful tool to persuade your customers to buy now not tomorrow. People tend to value more what they perceive as scarce or exclusive. How many times have you heard customers saying: I will come another time, I will come with my husband, wife, kids, friends etc. Applying this principle encourages your customers to make quick decisions. The quicker decisions are made, the sooner you can have your customer who is waiting to be served. This probably has happened to you. You went to liquor store, and when you saw that only few of your favourite wines left, it created urgency on you to buy it rather than coming another time to buy. This principle is an important psychological activator that uses shortage of quantities to make us act quickly. People automatically think that if something is scarce, it is because everyone wants it and if everyone wants it, it is because it should be good. According to Dr. Cialdini, the power of scarcity is divided into two factors:

1. People think that scare products at even higher price tend to be higher quality: For example, **Tesla partnered with a surf company and created 200 surfboards. The sale tag was $1500 before taxes. It was sold out quickly.**

2. People fear of losing a product that is scare: For example, **the Chinese phone maker Xiaomi launched their first phone in India with limited quantities (90,000 units). They were sold out in 13 seconds.**

Consequences of scarcity:

*Scarcity creates value what you sell.

* It creates a greater social demand.

* It allows stimulating your sale faster.

Some other examples of scarcity:

* Deciding to buy a plane ticket now because there are only few seats left.

* You go to Amazon website and you see the product you are interested have only few left.

*You book a room at hotel because there a few rooms left. As you see in these two pictures below, Ryan Air shows how many seats are left to create urgency on customers. In another example, Expedia applies this principle when you look for hotels in their website:

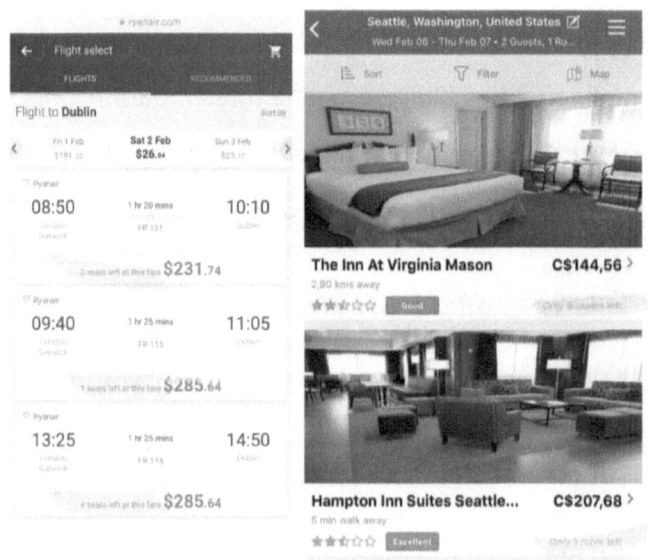

Two ways to create scarcity:

1. Limited quantities
2. Using deadlines

1. Limited quantities:

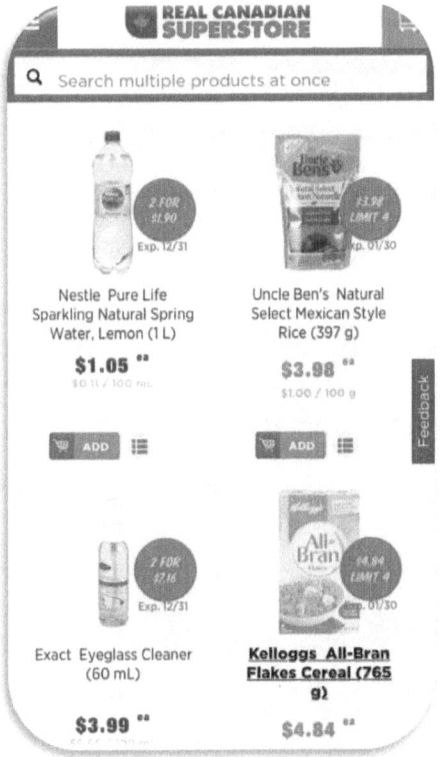

As you see in the pic, Superstore in Canada knows how to limit its products to create urgency on its customers.

People are all more motivated to buy a product that they think they can lose to buy. When people think that they have limited quantities, they condition themselves to make decisions quicker.

If you have products with limited quantities available, then you can use this principle to close your sales faster.

For example, when I worked in furniture store, they had piles of reserved and sold out stickers on mattresses on top shelves next to warehouse. When customers entered our store, the first thing they were seeing those mattresses with sold and reserved stickers on them.

You can apply limited quantity option with two methods:

1. You tell your customers that you got only a few left in the stock and they are not coming in upcoming days.

2. You tell your customer that I am not even sure that if we have this in stock because it is being sold fast so you call your friend and ask him that how many of that product in your stock. Of course, you expect your friend to say only a few left. If there are more in the stock, then there is no need to call your friend. The company I worked before had only one or two left rule. Wherever you called your friend to ask how many left, the other

salesperson had to say one or two left. Don't be like them and be honest what you say, if you have a lot of left, just say that we are selling this fast even if we have some in stock.

The later company I worked which was a competition of my previous company did not have this principle. Their closing ratio sucked big time comparing with my previous company even if they were bigger company than my previous company. They did not even have the principle of scarcity in their training. I had salespeople telling customers: we have many of it in stock. When you come back, I am sure we will have some in stock for you. Don't be like him. I will give you another example for limited quantities. A famous Turkish writer wrote a book and only published 1881 copies, which happens to be the birthday of Turkey's founder, Ataturk. The author sold all of his books in 30 minutes for 2500 liras ($400) each. People knew that the book was published in limited quantities and would be sold out quickly. Scarcity and fear of losing the opportunity to own the book created a sense of higher value and people were willing to pay a higher price than they normally would.

2. Using deadlines:

Informing your customers that the offer is only valid for a limited period of time also create urgency on customers. If you tell your customers that they have to make a decision quickly, because price is going to change, it awakens their fear of losing. Amazon informs its customers when the sales are ending to create urgency with time deadline as you see in the picture:

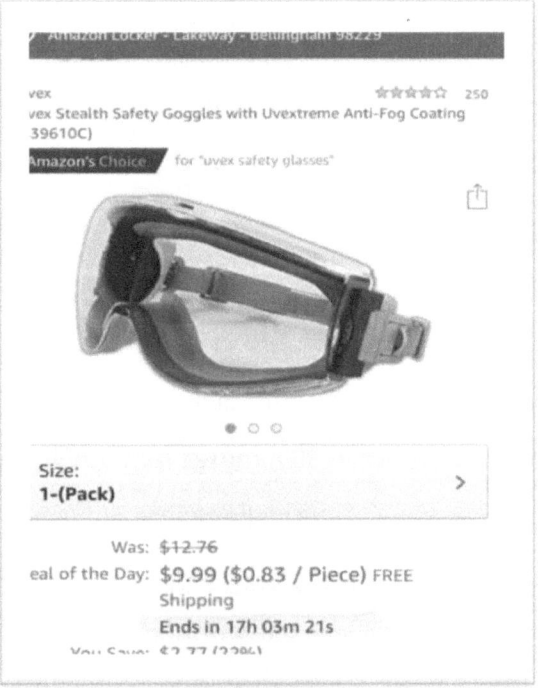

For example, I had a dentist customer who came to buy an appliance package that was on sale. He said he would come back next week. I told him that you are lucky now because it is on sale now and the price is going to change tomorrow morning. I urged him to buy now and he bought the package after showing him how much he could save if he buys it now.

Aware of adverse effects:

Firstly, if you force with pressure, the principle of scarcity to your customers, it can create an adverse effect on them. Secondly, generating urgency is fine, but lying to your customers is not a good idea. Do not pretend that you are giving a discount to customer for a product which is already on sale and discounted by your company. Thirdly, this principle should be used with caution because if you use abuse and use aggressive techniques, it can put you and your company at risk. Scarcity has to make sense. If you are going to create something artificial that does not make any sense for your customers, you will lose credibility on your customers. If there is no limited quantity, nor deadline for price change, then it is better not to use this method but just say: this product is selling fast since it is on sale or we have one centralized distribution depot and all of our stores order from the same distribution center so this product or products may be sold out in any given moment etc.

Creating scarcity with creating competition:

We had VIP sales events. These events usually were for one day deals. I used to invite customers on row by giving them appointments in close times with each other. I was also keeping their contact information and the products they were interested in buying. For example, I used to invite customers in different times .For example, I used to invite one on Saturday at 2:00 pm, other one on Saturday 2:15 pm, other one on Saturday at 2:30pm. I used to also make sure that they will come so I was calling them one or two days ago in advance. They used to come and they used to see that I was selling my customers while they were waiting for me and they were jumping into buying spree. When customers see that your product along with your service is good and demanded by other people, it also increases their desire to own it. Your objective in this technique should be increasing the degree of difficulty in accessing your service that increases your products' desirability. In addition all above, when they wait for you to be served, you should let them know that you will be with them shortly after finishing with your customers.

Creating scarcity by focusing on exclusivity:

Sometimes, your company may sell exclusive products. These types of products could be limited quantity and they are only sold in your store. You can focus on exclusivity to create scarcity in these products because this is a great opportunity for you to sell since nobody sells these types of products. We are good and so manufacturer only has chosen us over other stores to sell this product or their products etc.

Summary: As salesperson, you must use this well-known principle to awaken your customers' desire and urge them to buy now not tomorrow. Always try to close today, there is no tomorrow in sales.

Chapter 24: The Six-Step Selling Cycle

There are only six basic steps to sell your products to your customers. I could add retaining old customers as step 7 but I am talking about your current customers who come into your store to buy today. Think of these 6 steps when you date with someone:

Step 1: You meet with your partner at somewhere. She and you smile to each other. You ask him or her to go out a date at a restaurant. (Greetings)

Step 2: You meet at a restaurant and both of you learn about each other while eating. (Building rapport)

Step 3: You ask each other questions about each other's lives and what you expect from your relation.(Discover needs)

Step 4: You present yourself to her/him to show that you are ideal match for her/him. You try to impress on her/him with your speech and knowing what you expect from him/her in a relationship.

Step 5: You sometimes argue with your partner and you try to overcome her/his objections. Maybe you take him/her to a dinner to make things cooler again or you bring her/him a gift to cool things down. (Overcoming objections)

Step 6: After months or years have passed, both of you get marry and you start living together. (Closing)

Don't make these basic sales steps complicated: be simple as much as you can. Don't overload your customers with too much information. Don't forget that sales are not rocket science. Keep it simple as much as you can.

Step 1: Greetings

Greeting customers when they come into your store must be done with enthusiasm, passion and most importantly with a smile with eye contact to help them. Smiling to customers will help you also build a good rapport. Regardless of the nature of your day good or bad or your business, do not stop smiling at your customers when you greet them. If you do not know how to smile or if you cannot smile then, it will be harder for you for next steps in sales process. Smiling at customers makes you look more pleasant and accessible. If you want to impress and influence your customers to build a personalized relationship, this is the first step is that you should greet them with enthusiasm and with full of energy by having cheeky smile on your face. You must show a genuine interest in them as soon as they get into your store. This is the step where they will start to measure your credibility.

Smiling to your customers will also help you break ice with and will build up honesty and trust on their eyes about you. When you greet your customer with a good smile, you already started to sell something: Yourself and your smile. Smiling to them also make them relaxer if they are having a bad day. Lastly, smiling to your customers make them think that you are positive and give them a positive energy.

Don't do these below:

* Keep the distance with your customers. Don't get too close to them when you greet them.

* If you miss the opportunity to greet your customer immediately, you can slowly approach them and greet them. First impressions are important, especially the first five seconds. Don't run to customers like an athlete. Bad sales people do that and it looks very awkward and unprofessional. I had a salesman working with me. He was new into sales. As soon as he saw a customer coming into store, he walked to them so fast that customers were taken aback by his behaviour. You cannot build good rapport by doing this. You are not a child, but professional salesperson. Be professional, and mind your pace.

*If you miss greeting your customers, don't talk them from far ahead. For example, once, I went to a major clothing store. I wear extra-large and I started to check sweaters in my size. At the entrance, nobody greeted me.

A salesman saw me and from 10 feet away he said, "No, they won't fit you!" with a disapproving facial expression. After he said that, I stopped looking and left the store without saying anything to him. He is a good example how a bad sales person can make a customer leave the store. Bad rapport disconnects you from your customers. If your first impression with a customer is bad, it will be more difficult to build good rapport later on. When you greet customers with a smile without eye contact will look like: trying to make a pizza without dough. You must make sure that you do eye contact when you smile in greeting. Eye contact has the power to ignite or deepen a relationship that you will need to build a good rapport in other steps also.

Be careful when you do eye contact with your customer:

If you do too much eye contact, they may see you as an aggressive salesperson and if you do too little, they can think that you do not greet them with interest. Break your eye contact for each 5 seconds. Greet the customer with an appropriate greeting. Be aware of the time of day so you can greet him properly. For example, "Good morning," "Good afternoon," or, "Good evening." Mix a little talk about the weather to find a way to get closer to the customer. Talking about weather is a great step to build to personalized relationship with you customers.

- Hello, what a nice weather, what brings you in this nice weather?
- What brings you in aside from the cold weather?

Some other greeting examples:

Interest arising greeting:

You: Hello how are you doing in this cold day?
Customer: We are good thank you.

You: I feel like that I have seen you before.

Recognizing a previous customer:

You: Hello Michael, it is nice to see you back again. How are you?

Compliments in greeting:

Hello, how are you this beautiful afternoon?

Customer: I am fine thanks.

You: You look great today. I liked scarf on you.

Or you can say: you look classy today with nice suit on you.

Opportunistic greeting:

You: Hello, welcome to our store.

How are you doing today?

Customer: I do not feel good. I have a terrible headache.

You: I am so sorry. I had a terrible headache yesterday too. I got a Tylenol. If you would like to take one, I will bring it to you with water. Would you like to have it?

Humour in greetings:

You can use humour when you greet them. Humour actually should be used in all of sales process because humour is a way of relaxing people and can easily put them in a good mood.

You: Hello, how are you? (It is too cold outside and you can see that customer was shivering) Customer: We are fine, but it is too cold outside.

You: Yes it is very cold outside but you are lucky because you are at our store now. We will keep you warm inside.

Formal greeting:

You: Hello, how are you?

Customer: We are fine, thank you.

You: Good, how can I help you today? Find out the customer's name. People in general like to be called by their names. It is a good idea to use their first name. This is the time you can shake your customers' hands. Shake their hands and introduce yourself. If you miss this step, you can do it in second step. Keep the conversation light and casual at first. Don't talk about products right away after greeting them. You can use casual topics to talk to customer. Humour is a good tool to put your customer at ease. Humour can be used in all stages of the sales process.

Summary:

There are variety methods and styles in greetings. You can develop your own styles. You should try to get attention from your customers with your greetings. If you cannot make them attentive in your greetings, the next sale steps will be harder to break ice with your customers. Don't be like those politicians: Too serious. Smile, and use humour if you can.

Step 2: Building Rapport: If I had one choice to choose what step is the most important one would be out of 7 steps, I would definitely say building rapport. In this step, you try to impress your customers and sell yourself to them as an exemplary sales person.

I added 4 people in the picture. These four people come from different backgrounds. Their clothes, works, looking and behaviours are totally different than each other. Your sales pitch with Tom may not work with Lisa and your sales pitch Michael may not work with Celine. You must be like chameleon in this step. Change your sales pitch and your game plan for each customer you see in the pic and you see in your sales floor. Talk to Tom about how his farming business goes and how he does this year. Talk to Lisa about how her studies going, what she takes. People like to be listened and they liked to be paid attention to their lives. If you do this step properly, you can sell almost anything you want to your customer. You should read the Principle of Likability very well to build a personalized rapport and you must be like chameleons: changing your sales pitch and behaviours for each customer differently. That's why, I put the Principle of Likability at the beginning of the book. You will start to apply the principle of likability in this step. This is the step where you will start to sell truly yourself to your customers. If you can have a good impression in step 1, this step will be easier for you to build a personalized relationship with your customers. If you can build a personalized, friendly and an impressive with your customers:

- They will trust you.

- They will see that you are a confident salesperson and knowing what you sell.
- It is going to be so easy to overcome their objections.
- You are going to sell almost anything.

  You cannot sell anything at any price without selling yourself first. This is the step when you will learn about your customers and when they will learn about you

  If you make them like you when you build rapport with them, then not only building a good rapport with them will lessen their objections to buy from you but also you will sell whatever you want to sell according to their needs.

  Asking questions your customers will help you build rapport faster. For example, you will ask personalized questions about them and show them your curiosity about their answers
- You: Where do you work?
- Customer: At X Restaurant
- You: Cool, I have some customers working there, Jack just was here to buy last week.(Jack works there) I been there last well. You guys do great service.

- You: Where do you live?
- Customer: X town.
- You: Cool, I was there last week. It is very nice place to be. Do you know Thomas? He lives there too. He is my customer. Ask questions, and let them talk. The more they can talk about something, the more similarities you can find with them. Try to personalize your conservation with them as much as much you can. Look at the life from their angle and let them talk and show your curiosity about their talk while asking questions. Don't talk about your products or about yourself in this step because you are trying to sell yourself at this step. This is an introductory step in where you try to get your customers attention.

Step 3: Discover their needs:

Now, we are at step three where you will learn truly why customers are in our store. In this part, you will ask a lot of questions. Asking questions will help you discover true needs and expectations of your customers.

Use a simple language: Don't use complicated language when you ask questions to certain customers. You do not know yet if your customers know about the product technicalities. For example, not everybody has technical understanding about TVs. If your customer does not anything about TVs, asking questions below will make them confused:

* Would you like to have LED, LCD, or OLED Tv?
* Would you like to have UHD, or HD?
* Would you like to have a smart TV or not?
* Would you like to have Dolby Vision?

Instead of asking those questions above, you can ask:

* What size are you looking for?
* What type of TV do you have at home? (Then you can figure out if they liked it or not)
* What happened to your current TV?(If they said it stopped working, then this is an opportunity to sell extended warranty later on)
* Do you have any preference?
* Is it for living room or spare room? (People usually do not want to spend much for their living room)
* What do you do you mostly on TV? Watching movies, watching sport games or playing games or something else?

Asking right questions related with the product will save you and your customers' time. Asking questions you will narrow product choices to show them. The less suitable product you show them, the more time you will save in your sales. For example, you have a young customer who seems knowing about TVs. You asked the size and he said 65-inch TV. You have only 10 pieces 65-inch TV and only you have 8 of them on display. So you narrowed your choices to 8 TVs.

You have to narrow it more:

Will you watch Netflix or go to internet on it? He said I will watch Netflix. That means a smart TV he needs. You have 5 smart TVs on display. Your choices dropped to 5 from 8. Now, you have 5 TVs to show him. Your target should be always eliminating your choices to up to 3. Pick up those 3 TVs in your mind and start showing these 3 TVs from the most expensive to the least expensive. It is always easier to go down from the most expensive one to the least expensive one. "Don't ask if you have any budget, or price range. Most of sales people do that. Asking the customers what price range they are looking for is not a good starting point to check their price range. You can learn their budget when you start to show the most expensive TV among those 3 TVs."

Summary:

Asking qualifying questions that will help you determine the needs and wants of the customer. Asking qualifying questions will also help you understand that if your customers are really interested in buying today or they are just checking. Ask these qualifying questions for the all products you sell. Don't show all of your products to your customers. Show what you have on your display and what you think it is best for them. Try to sell what you have on your display or in your store which is not displayed. It is easier to sell products that you have in your store than what you have online your company's website. You may not have some TVs on display or you may have some TVs in your website but not in your store. In these circumstances, show customers similar TVs that have similar features in step 4. It will help you and them save valuable time. If you cannot ask right qualification questions, you will circle around to show them many different products. You will waste your time and their time.

Step 4: Presentation

Knowledge is a power and money. You can be the most educated person in your store. It does not matter. You can have an MBA in sales. It does not matter. You can be the best sales person who has the product knowledge in your store. It does not matter unless you do not an impressive presentation to influence your customers. In this number four step, you must show your customers your expertise with valuable knowledge and skills you possess to present the products. Presenting your products are like a dance singers singing in theatre. If you cannot sing well, then you will disappoint your audiences. So, you must demonstrate your customers that you know what you sell. If you cannot demonstrate that you don't know about your products, you will lose your credibility. Don't forget golden rule. The more products you show them, the more you will confuse them. The more products you show them, the more time you and they will spend. Control your sale and limit your choices according to their answers in step 3. You are the salesperson and you decide what could be the best for your customers according to their needs. You must be like a commander in battlefield. You should give your customer confidence on your presentation and give the confidence that you have a total control of your sale. Showing many products and making them confused will help nothing but make them more undecided to buy.

Some of customers know what they want or what they need but they may have trouble expressing it on their own. Most of them will not know which product could be the best for them. Asking right questions with a simple language will remove the barriers for them to understand features of the products. Be simple as is.

From Step 1 to Step 6, always try to exclude price talks from your conservation.

During the presentation, you should have and focus on:

1. Product knowledge

2. Explain Features and benefits by creating value

3. Have passion and enthusiasm about your products

4. Use the Sense of Touch

5. Communication skills

1: Product knowledge:

You need to show your skills and knowledge about product knowledge with customer. Knowing your products well builds confidence on your customers and having product knowledge helps you to deliver excellent presentation. Customers can understand that you do not know much about the product you are selling and they can lose confidence about you and it will very hard at this point to regain your confidence. If you are new hire and if you don't have product knowledge about all products you sell, just focus on certain products at first and excel on them to show your customers. If you don't know about your product, don't pretend that you know. If you cannot answer a question, ask some of your co-workers.

2. Features and benefits

If you can explain features and benefits to your customers well, you will have less resistance for price objections. Features are basically what something is or made of and benefits are what something does. Features could be specs, size, and dimensions:

- Mattress size.
- Fabric type of sofa.
- Traction control in your car.

The benefits are that what that product makes for them:

This mattress is king size (Feature). There is a lot of space for you to sleep with your partner (Benefit).

-This sofa is made of genuine leather (Feature).Leather is very easy to be maintained and it will make easier you ton wipe off your pets' fur (Benefit)

I will give you an out of retail sales example:

If you were and a car salesman and told your customer: This car has dynamic latest technology traction control.(**Feature**)What would your customer think? Does everybody know what dynamic traction control? Having dynamic traction control is a feature and customers don't buy features.

After mentioning traction control, if you said: This dynamic traction control regulate your car's traction on icy&snowy conditions and enable sport style driving while providing you active stability control. If the rear wheels are stuck in snow and if they cannot spin properly, this leads to slip on the front wheels. This dynamic traction reduces the power on rear wheels to keep you on the road again to keep you and your kids safe during driving. (Benefits)I used to see salespeople who say: our product is the best, this is the best product we have. Telling them this product is the best is a vague term. Customers do not care what the best is. They care about what the best product can do for them.It is difficult to sell effectively if you cannot show all features and the benefits of a particular product against the needs of buyers. For example, if your customer has back pain, then tell your customer why this mattress is good for him and how it will help him to reduce his back pain. Dear customer this customer has advanced pocket coil technology, they are independent from each other as if independent car suspensions (Features). When you move around the mattress, your partner is not disturbed. Also, since they are independent from each other, they support your back all the time (Benefits). You can also explain features and benefits by comparing two similar products. Your customer already told you that his machine was making too much noise. This is opportunity for you to sell more expensive washing machine because it has a noise reduction technology that cheaper machine you already showed to your customer did not have: Mr. Customer, this washer has Direct Drive Motor Technology. Conventional washers as the one you are interested, have only a belt and they only rotate to one direction. In time the belt loosens and gives off. In addition those conventional machines make more noise because of the belt. In this new Direct Drive Motor Technology, there is no belt. (Feature). So you do not need to worry about your machine will stop working when belt gives off (Benefit). This technology also makes washing your clothes quieter and more energy efficient to save you money (Benefit).I already mentioned you that conventional machines rotate to only one direction but this Direct Drive Technology has six rotating option(Feature).These rotation options wash your clothes more efficiently. You do not even to worry about rotation options. The machine decides automatically what rotating option is optimal according to what you wash (Benefit).Knowing your products well will help build trust between you and your customers. Customers like credibility. You do not have product knowledge then you will lose your credibility. You must try to create a value for the product you are selling: Value is not something tangible. Value is what your customers perceive about your products. To decide about purchasing a product, a customer will value a product's benefit higher than its function. For example, a customer doesn't buy a coffee table just to decorate her room. She buys coffee table to put something on it. Customer perceived value usually has little to do with actual price. It is perceived benefit of your product. You can easily create value by explaining them why your product is good for them and what your product will make for them. When your customers compare the difference between perceived benefit and perceived cost, they weight benefits&features. If they perceive value is higher to benefit, customers will have a positive surplus in benefits comparing with features. If you can create value, you can even sell plastic surgery to an old celebrity or you can sell even oil to a Saudi. If you can create value, you can sell any product at your price to any customers on condition that you had built a personalized rapport. If you cannot create value, you may still sell but they may return it, or you will not have long term relationship with them. Creating value on what you sell will make your customers to take their money out their wallet easier and without thinking.

3. Have passion and enthusiasm about your products: You should have passion and enthusiasm about the product. Doing presentation with passion and enthusiasm will generate customer's enthusiasm about the product. A good product knowledge increases motivation in you and this enthusiasm will spread to your customer.

4. Use the Sense of Touch

Would you buy shoes or pants without trying? Would

you buy a car without test drive? Would you get marry to someone without knowing her/him well? Probably not. Unfortunately, most of salespeople do not know how to make their customers feel the product. Letting them to touch, sit, lay down on the products you sell increase their perceived ownership. If you are trying to sell a mattress, let them lay down, turn around etc. If you are trying to sell, give the remote control to your customer to change channels and play with the buttons. If you are trying to sell a fridge, let them open the door, play with buttons, shelves etc. Tactile sensations are very important to create a sense of ownership to sell your products. Don't let them look at your products from the distance as new lovers look at each other, let them touch what you sell.

5. **Communication skills**

   Use always a simple language. You cannot tell an old couple: this TV has 200Hz. You know what it means for you but most of customers don't know what it is. This TV has 200Hz. Having 200Hz means that you can watch fast-moving sports without having motion blur and if your grandchildren comes at you to play games, they will have processing speed to play their games without freezing on them.

During the presentation:

- Keep eye contact and break it each 5 seconds(you should do this in sales steps)
- Facial expressions: smiling, raising your eyebrows
- Verbal confirmation: reflecting what they say.
- Body postures: match their postures
- The rhythm of their breath: Matching their breathing their phase.
- Tone of the voice: Match their tone not to show them that you are in the same phase.

Summary:

You should aim at making them to pay attention to your presentation. You need to make an effective and impactful presentation for them to listen to you. No matter how advanced you are in your career, you need to polish, and decorate your presentation with examples. If you see that your customers are getting boring, you can change the subject or use humour to make them relax. Don't forget every customer is different and not all of them eat rice. Watch your time frame during presentation. The more time you take, the less information they will have in their mind. Try to keep it short as much as you can and always mention them: this isn't going to take very long before starting to presentation. People don't like taking too much time during the presentations.

Writing long sentences is like adding water to tea; the more words, the weaker the message."-Dianna Booher

Step 5: Objections

For sales people, having customer rejections and getting "no's" from our customers is our daily occurrence. The sales without objections do not exist. If nobody objected, we would be a millionaire now. Moreover, if we let every customer leave with no's then we would not be a salesman. The ability to overcome objections is critical, because the result depends on our persuasion skills. I have had many salespeople when their customers had objections they were getting nervous and shaking. You must be calm, be relax and listen to them to understand their objections clearly.

Types of customer objections:

Price: The biggest objections of the customers are the price. If the price plays a decisive and critical role in your customers' objections, and as salesperson if you do not know how to overcome this most important objection, how to defend your price and negotiate the price of your product, you will have serious sales problem. It is logical that the customers want to get what they want with the lowest price. Overcoming price objections is will be your bread and butter. It is what makes this job so interesting and challenging. You should see the price objections as an opportunity to explain benefits of your product in a different way. When you are handling price objections, you should not be offended. Customers may think it is too expensive. Don't be offended. Empathize with your customer and try to understand why they think that it is expensive for them. "It is too much. I will think about that. I'm really interested but I think I can get cheaper somewhere else. "You have heard, hear and will hear these types of statements from customers all the time. As professional salesperson, you must always be prepared price objection with ready responses to those questions above. You must develop techniques and responses for different scenarios. Developing techniques and ready responses will make you more flexible, adaptable, efficient and confident. Overcoming objections is an opportunity for you to develop and improve your sales skills. Bad sales pitches from bad salespeople may cause customer objections. As salesperson, you cannot ruin a good product with a bad pitch. Bad salespeople are one of the biggest consequences for customer objections because they could not create a value for the products which increases customers' objections and causes giving them discounts.

Price objection could be real: They really do not have enough money to buy your product. If you can build a good personal rapport with customers, you can figure out if their price objection is real or unreal. If your customer is on welfare, then big chance price objection is real or she is single mother with 3 children. You always ask what their jobs are. Then, you can illustrate in your mind how much they make and plan your sales steps. For example, I always used to show the most expensive item first to see if they have price objections right away.

Price objection could be unreal: they have money to buy your product but either it wants to get better deal or it is above their spending purchase. In this situation, you must create a value on the product to reduce the price objection and eliminate it completely. You probably have heard tons of times if you are in sales for a long time and you will hear tons of times if you are new in sales, customer saying:

* **This product is too expensive. (TV)**

There are many different ways to answer your customers when price is expensive for them. Depends on how you already built rapport with them, try to get personal with them. You can use humour or give comparative examples. Make it simple when you give examples.

For example, **dear customer there is tomatoes with $2 and there are tomatoes with $3. Both are red but the first one does not have the same taste like the latter one. The latter one has more protein, the more fibre and tastier than cheaper one. People do love these types of real life examples.**

Compare your product with another similar product to overcome price objection:

For example: **You are trying to persuade your customer to buy $2500.00 4K UHD TV. You told me that you will watch sport games on your TV and you have sometimes** guess coming into your home to watch your wonderful Seattle Seahawks team. (Always call your customers with their name)This TV has instantaneous response time which means it does not have motion blur. It has also wide viewing angles so when your friends come over to watch your team's game, they can view the game from any angle. The previous TV I showed you do not have this feature. Show him some small numbers to reduce price in his mind. Making numbers smaller can be an effective trick. Paying $2500 could be seen a big price for TV. I understand you. We do not buy TV often as we buy groceries every day or every week. There is only $500 difference between these two and average lifetime of the TV is 10 years. So you will pay only $.13 cents daily difference more to have this TV. ($500/3650 days=$.13)You will only pay $.36 to have this TV in total daily. ($2500/3650=$.68). What is $.68? We cannot even buy a cup of coffee with it.

* **My friend bought it cheaper before:** Mr. Customer I do not know if he bought exactly this TV or another one but as far as I know that this TV has never been at lower price. Maybe he bought another version of this TV. Now, let's make it harder and let's supposed that your customer called his friend and asked him TV model.It is one lower model of the TV that you are trying to sell but he still is continuing to resist the price. This TV has these features and benefits but your friend's TV does not have. (You differentiate two TVs by focusing on benefits) I have also good news for you. We have 90 days price guarantee which most stores do not have. If the price drops down, we will match the price in 90 days.There are too many scenarios and solutions to handle price objections. You will develop your own solutions in time.

Create scarcity: **This TV is selling fast at the moment because it is on first page of our flyer. When I checked in the morning, we had only 4 left. I will check something for you. (Don't tell your customer you will check stock levels, he may reject you right away).You leave from the customer and pretend you are checking your stock levels or check your stock levels really if you do not know how many left) Go back to your customer with a happy face and say:I have great news for you. There are only 3 left. Tomorrow is weekend so it is going to be sold out tomorrow. Since NFL season starting next week, there is a lot of demand on 4K UHD TVs, so we already sold for 20 of these TV. Sport funs love 4K TVs like this with UHD. I also checked that TV** will be on backorder for next three weeks. Telling your customer TV will be on back order and telling him a lot of sport fans buy this TV creates urgency and social validation in his eyes. When you say, sport fans prefer to buy this TV; customers think that if they buy it, it should be good. Using scarcity is an important tool to overcome price objections.

Price objections stemming from competition: **When I used to sell furniture, there was furniture in the town. We had a lot of customers who were saying about this X store:**

- My friend bought it at X store.

- This product is at X price over there.

- I will go and I will check what X has to offer.

- They have free delivery at X store.

Overcoming competition objections is not hard they were the easiest ones I used to overcome. I did everything to keep those customers to shop in our store. I hated giving discounts but I gave discounts in rare occasions to keep them in our store. I had a customer who wanted to buy

$20,000 worth products for her new house. It was her visit to our store. She would go to competition after us. No way, I could let her go to competition. She said I was hungry, I said no big deal. I ordered pizza for her. She said I was thirsty; I brought water and made coffee with her. She said I wanted to go to washroom. I accompanied her to washroom and opened the door for her. She said I had not had enough money to buy now. I offered her financing with no interest for 18 months. Finally, I sold her whatever she wanted to buy. She spent $26,500! Regardless of their competition objections, you should prevent them going to competition. You don't want make those guys making money over there. You want your company and yourself to make money. Always focus on why you are better than competition and focus on your qualities and better services. Don't use the word "competition" and their name with your customers. You focus on your company's strengths and why it is better to buy from you. Don't bash your competition or their products. Don't even talk about them. Be like a politician, play dumb when it is necessary. **Last strike**: whatever you did, whatever explained, if you still cannot overcome price objections, try to get some small commitments from your customers. For example, you can get a small deposit by telling the price you will lock the price increase, or offer them your financing options(you can offer this before too).Again, if you close the sale, get their phone number to call them back.

Some other important objections:

* Time objections: They could be moving to their new house 6 months later and they are not fully ready to buy. They are just checking around. Focus on availability of your products, and try to get layaway deposit or full payment and offer them that you will bring their products in exact date they want to pick up or delivered.

* Old habits: They could be reluctant to change old habits. You did not have brand or design you wanted to have so they are reluctant to buy something they are not familiar with. Focus on benefits of having this new brand comparing what their older ones do not have and what this one has and does for them. Don't bash nor say bad things about their current product. For example, if they are at you to buy a Samsung washer, if you do not have Samsung washer, don't tell them that Samsung makes awful washers.

* Trust: You could not give them enough credibility in your sales steps so they are having hard time to trust your expertise. This is hard one to overcome. You and your customer together walked from Step 1 to Step 5 and you could not give them credibility. At this point, this will be harder for you to give them credibility because you missed giving them credibility in first 4 steps. In this situation, you should turn the sales to one of your co-workers or show the customer a video or a brochure to make them believe. If you have turn over sales technique in your store, call your friend and introduce him or her with your customer. Tell your customer that my friend X has some important additions and he is going to help you out with his years' experience.

Important points to overcome objections:

These are some important points when customer has objections:

* <u>Listen</u>: Listen to your customers. You must allow them to express themselves. Listening to them actively also can give you hints to reduce objections.

* <u>Be calm</u>: There are tons of bad sales people out there that get angry when customer says this is too expensive. I had a salesman who told the customer to buy at Thrift

Store if the price is too expensive. Don't be like him. Be calm; don't use ironies or mocking words.

* <u>Do not interrupt</u>: Don't interrupt your customers when they are expressing their objections.

* <u>Do empathy and never deny their objections</u>: If you do then, customer may be offended or they can stop listening to you. Don't avoid, nor ignore objections. Objections must always be answered without arguing with your customers.

* <u>Answer objections clearly and with simplicity</u>: Don't use complicated sentences. Don't answer questions in an uncertain way or without knowing the answer. In addition that doesn't lie to overcome objections.

* <u>Ask questions</u>: It is important to ask questions. Do not use taboo word like expensive when you ask questions.

* <u>Use I statements</u>: Using I statements help you create a common ground with your customers. It gives them impression that you understand the importance of their objections.

* <u>Keen on</u>: Show them that you keen on solving their objections by saying: "Let me see what I can do for you

about the price. Let me explain how I can solve this issue etc.

* Be comparative with out of product examples: I used this example a lot in my sales. The price of a luxury car like BMW is not the same with a Fiat car. Both take you from one spot to other one but the first one has more quality than the latter one.

* Try to create an individualized value: if there is one lemon left in the kitchen, you will share it the half with your wife because she needs the lemon to make salad. You need other half to use in your soup. Both of you need the lemon for different needs. Each customer can give different value for the same product. Focus in their differences not their similarities. A mattress with memory foam for a customer could be better for a customer and the same mattress for another customer could not a good choice. If you can create more individualized value by focusing on benefits, you will have higher chances to overcome objections.

* Generate options: If you cannot overcome price objections, you can also downgrade the product to another product. It is easier to go down from more expensive product to less expensive product.

*<u>Use handover technique</u>: Call one of your friends to handle price objections without offering them a discount. Your friend can explain your customer in a different way to overcome price objections.

Summary:

Handling and overcoming objections are the most challenging part of the sales. You are there to get their money and they are there to reduce the price or leaving without buying. Objections are a normal reflection of the customers. We want to influence them to overcome their objections and they resist buying. When you have objections, it is not generally bad. Having objections shows us that they have still interest in our products

Handling discounts: I will tell you the last thing as the first thing without rounding the words before explaining you why discount is not good thing. You should or you must use the discount option as last bullet in your sales arsenal to close the sale and you should only give discounts if your customers are about to leave from your store. Again, you should only give discounts if you see that they are going to leave without buying because price was too high for them. No matter how much you were good, no matter how your products are good, you will have customers who ask for discount or who think the price is too much for them. However, you can minimize giving discounts by some tricks. The techniques to prevent and reduce discounts:

Create value for your products:

Again, we need to talk about creating value. Giving discount creates devaluing your products. As professional salesperson, it is your responsibility not to sell the product but to sell the value of your products. Building value must be your number one priority to prevent discounts. If they still ask discount, try to build value in a different way as comparing similar products with the one you are selling. You need to focus on how your product or service can add value to your prospect's business. Most of customers value the products based on their price. I had a salesperson who told his customer when customer said that this sofa was too expensive for her to afford. He said: I know that it is too expensive, because it is the best sofa. If you say your customer as he did, then you will have difficulties to prevent discounts. If he said: **Quality products come at cost. This dining table is made of real wood, it is durable and all the gaps are filled with resins and epoxies that create a finish where the natural beauty of the wood shines through as you see (while telling this, if he told: you please touch in the table to see how gaps are filled and how it feels).

If he continued saying:I have laminate tables which are way cheaper than comparing this table. I can happily sell you a laminate dining table but it is made of synthetic materials. Since it is not made of from the wood, it is considered lower quality comparing with this table. Laminate table has shorter life expectancy comparing this real wood table. You will also be able to restore it in the future if you have scratches while you will not have this option in laminate table etc. You can also shortly give an example out of table. You told me that you drive Chevrolet Impala which is a higher model than Chevrolet Malibu because it is better made and it has some extras that Malibu does not have. This dining table is like your Impala etc.

Have confidence in you and in your products:

If you cannot have confidence in your product and in yourself, then you will increase your chances to be asked discounts. If you offer discount, your customer can lose confidence in your product and in you. You must stand what you are selling and try to sell wholeheartedly. Confidence is a very important game changer to prevent discounts and if you lost it. You will probably lose the sale or you will have to give discounts.

Use your time properly:

If you don't spend the proper amount of time with your customers, then you're going to have a much harder time closing that sale which can lead the price objections and discounts.

Show them your effort:

When I was a salesperson, I hated giving discounts and I never used "discount" name with my customers. Salespeople's wordings have so much impact on how customers perceive salespeople' discounts. Therefore, never ever don't use the word "discount". Remove it from your vocabulary. I used to use the words like price reduction, get $ off, savings etc. That you should always use. If they insisted on having discount, then I did not say them directly: let me see how much discount I can give you. I said words like let me see what I can do for you. Let me see if I can make you extra savings even if you are already saving a lot. I had variety different steps to avoid giving discounts. I will explain one of my effective steps that worked most of time.

A sofa sale that costs $1000:

1. When you see that your customer is about to leave by saying: they will come another time, or when they say, they will come back another time. Then, you say that I want you to save some money. I see that you think it is expensive and I will see what I can do for you.

2: You go to computer and pretend checking something on computer.

3: You go back and tell them: I have great news for you. You are lucky, we sell it almost at cost (If the product is already on sale), and you are getting the best price if you buy it now.

If your customer still resists, then you tell them that I will talk to my manager and be back in a few minutes. You go to your manager and ask him/her how much discount you can give to your customers, otherwise they will leave. Your manager says 25%, and you go back to your customers by saying: We did our best for you with my manager. You are a nice customer and nice people like you deserve saving more. I am going to make you save $150. My deal is $850 for you now and scratches the price with a huge cross to show her saving. Most of customer will take the deal and buy the sofa. If the customer says, it is not still much, and then you have a room to play. This technique does work. Customers see your effort to give them discount. Even if your manager told you to give $250, with this technique, you can make most of customers accept $150. If they don't, you still have room to play with the price. Don't go to your managers right away after customer asked discounts. They are usually busy and you should try to handle everything in your own in your sales as much as you can. As I mentioned you: firstly, go to computer to pretend that you are trying to do something for them to give discounts. If it does not work, then you can go to your manager. The more effort you show them to give discount, the less price objections they will have. They will see your effort and they will like it. Don't also show the costs of the products to your customers to try to prove that you really don't sell it expensive. Do use this technique, this technique does work!

Consequences of discounts:

When you offer a discount, your customer can tell their friends or relatives that they got discount from you and from your store. When you give discount to them, your customers will expect to see the same thing next time. You don't want to see precedent customers who ask you discount every time or their acquaintances. That is one of the last things you want to have in your sales or in your store. In addition that they will also place less value on your products and your store will have a name as discount store. You will also have less income and you must do more sales to hit your sales quotas due to discounts.

Summary:

If you give discounts, not only you thrash the value of your products but also it urges other customers asking discounts. If you cannot build a good rapport, if you cannot know well about your products, if you cannot have confidence in your presentation, then you will increase your customers asking discount. Don't devalue your products in your customers' mind. Don't take money from your paycheque to give discounts!

Step 6: Closing

Do you want to buy this?

Would you like to buy this?

I had many salespeople who asked these absurd closing questions. I know you will not be like them because you are reading this book. In closing you want to learn that your customer will buy or not. It is basically a to be or not a to be. If you ask questions which can be answered with yes or no, then you are putting all of effort at risk. According to sales force research, 73% of salespeople ask absurd closing questions. I know you want to be one out of 27%. **You must never ask any questions to your customers at closing that can be answered with yes or no.**

Signals to close the sale:

It is very important to know what the best moment is to close the sale. If you try so early to close the sale, you may lose it completely, if you try to close it so late, you may change your customers' mind and they may ask you more time to think about. Therefore, you should always listen to your customers and try to understand customer's facial gestures or expressions. If they look thoughtful, if they look excited, if they look happy, if they look smiley, then this is time for you to close the sale. There are a lot of techniques and tricks to do closing steps properly and efficiently. Every sales book or your training manual defines the closing techniques differently but their purpose is all the same: Close the sale and make that money. You must try to evade asking closing questions that either can end with a yes or with no. It is 50/50%. You must use a tactical approach to ask questions.

Some important closing techniques:

Soft Close: You mentioned that you were interested in delivery when I had asked you. I am sorry that I have forgotten checking delivery spot for upcoming days. We have been very busy lately and I don't think have delivery spot for the next week but since you are wonderful people, I will ask my manager to open up a delivery spot. Or you can say:

Jack I like the farmers like you. You guys feed us good (smile) Look at me, I got fat (by pointing your stomach and smile) or I eat healthy thanks your farmers like you. I know it is harvesting season now, so you will be busy. I will make sure that we will not interrupt your job. We will call you before coming and you just need to open the door for you. What date is the best for you to have delivery for Jack?

Commitment Close: There are only few products left in the stock. I will make sure that you will have your product on the time. Oh it is my mistake that I should reserve the product in cash register for a few minutes to make sure that nobody buys it before it. It happened to me once. I was about to process a sale, and someone else in another store bought this fridge before me because there was only one left.

Alternative Close: I forgot if we have the red colour in the stock. Red colour is sold a lot lately. Are you ok with yellow or do you like yellow?

Opinion closing: I liked the sofa. I need to get a sofa for my spare room too. Your guess will be impressed with it. By the way, I forgot that we have matching pillows for it. I got a perfect one that goes with this sofa (You bring the pillow instead of taking them back). If they don't say no, then that means the sale is closed and they are buying.

Direct Close: We can go to cash register to finish the process. By the way, we have financing options. If you would like to have, we can do financing. (You are just saying the financing option to find out if they are buying or not.

Opportunity cost close:

You can use this closing technique if they have higher chance to buy to eliminate their complete price objection. You can prove your customers how much money they will save if they buy certain products. For example, if they don't have energy efficient washer, and prove them how much they can save during the lifetime of washer. Mr. Michael average lifetime of a washer is 11 years. You can save up to between $ $70to $100 on water and on electricity with this washer. This energy efficient washers use up to 50% less water and up to 37% less energy. This washer consumes 316 kWh of electricity while yours uses between 410 kWh and 450 kWh energy. Would not you like to save money?

Closing by mistake: You make a mistake in details intentionally to see if they are buying or not. I made a small mistake. On Tuesdays, we don't do pickups because our truck comes from the distribution center. What about Wednesday? If they say no, then try to make an exception for customer. For example, on Tuesdays we did not have pick up for our customers since we had trucking coming. If it was our last chance to close the sale, we were making exception for the customers.

Imaginary closing:

I forgot asking that what colour of your living is? They say a colour and you say: I forgot mentioning you to show a matching carpet for this sofa. (Be silent for 5 seconds and wait if customer says yes or no for carpet).If customer says: we don't want carpet now, then, you closed the sale.

Price change closing:

I am sorry I just forgot checking something fast. I may have given you the old price. You quickly check the price and say: You are lucky today. I gave you the correct price. It happened to me once. I gave wrong price to customer and I had to honour my price. It was busy today. I think I should take the break after you. By the way, how will you pay today?

Using humour in closing:

I used humour from step 1 to step 6 in all of my sales. If you don't use humour in first 5 steps, be careful when you use humour in closing. What a lucky person you are today. You dealt with me and you are saving $ amount from these products. Which restaurant do you go usually? Customer says X restaurant. Well, you saved that much money today shopping at us and from me. Now, you can go to your restaurant that xx times and eat free food thanks to your saving you had at us. (You can use something else instead of restaurant too). Would you like to save more money? (You ask customer with a smiley face).

Summary: Closing sales are the most exciting part of sales process. Because you know that money is your pocket. Every customer is different. All of them have different needs, personalities. Closing a sale successfully depend on your success in previous steps. In closing, customer should not even feel that you are closing the sale. There is a famous player called Messi that plays for Barcelona. He is considered one of the best players in the world. In 90 minutes soccer game, you will only see Messi when he assists or scores or doing some important contribution to the game. He will be only noticed in the most important actions in the game. So the closing your sale is a must.it does not matter how you served your customers well, how they liked you but it matters to sell now. Once they are out of store, nobody will give you guarantee they will come back to you. Another sharp sales person in your competition may steal your sales. It is to be or not to be, it is to make that money or not. Do your steps correctly, you will close your sales successfully. Think of these 6 steps like a sport game, like a chess game, like a war game. Plan ahead and execute.

The Summary

I do not give you guarantee that I am the best writer. With limited English, I did my best and I compiled important subjects that will lead that you success. As an immigrant sales person on the floor, I used my accent in my advantage to close the sales and I was very successful on it. I was beating in the most experienced sales people in any company I worked even at my first months because I learned that the sales is a complete game. From the second they get into your store, you must play your game according the rules I wrote in this book.

> The sales is a complete game. If I was asked my opinion, what it takes to be the best sales person, I would say the six below. Of course, I do not want to mean that other subjects in this book are not important. All of them are important but the ones below are going to take you to success in your career. Rule of Thumb: Always try to close you sales today, have confidence and below any tactics or tricks you learned in this book or from your friends or from your training manual. There is no tomorrow in sales, there is always today. CLOSE TODAY, NOT TOMORROW and Always try to be POSITIVE, CONFIDENT and RESILLIENT in any circumstances.

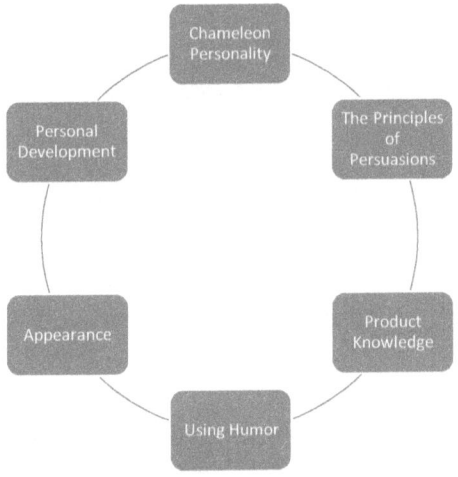

The End

www.ingramcontent.com/pod-product-compliance
Lightning Source LLC
Chambersburg PA
CBHW031610210526
45464CB00004B/1507